FROM SNOW
TO SUNSHINE

IRENA SIKORSKA

FROM SNOW TO SUNSHINE

Routh Lodge Press

LONDON 2007

Published by
ROUTH LODGE PRESS
Routh Lodge
London
SW18 3SW

Printed in Great Britain
by POLPRINT
63 Jeddo Road, London W12 9EE

Typesetting: Marek Czubek

ISBN 978-0-9554215-0-1

Acknowledgements

I am indebted to Liz Philpot who inspired me to put down on paper some of my past, poetically described by her: From Snow to Sunshine.

To Lora and Friderich Ragette for their encouragement and support in the realisation of this work.

To Pierre Ratcliffe for his indefatigable research into the background information contained in the appendices, and some useful additions.

To Eva Skelley for editing the text.

Cover design: Elisabeth Ratcliffe

From the author

I was born in 1925 in North–East of Poland, near Wilno. After the outbreak of the Second World War in 1939 I shared for nine years the unfortunate fate of so many Polish people. The Russians deported us beyond the Ural mountains. Later I reached a refugee camp in Teheran under the care of UNRRA. Then I was directed to Polish settlements at Koja in Uganda. Finally, in 1948, I arrived with my mother and my brothers in England where we were united with my father. My life as a fully independent citizen of the free world followed a peaceful, but exciting, path. First, as a student, then my professional career as an architect; marriage and family life. Throughout my adult life I craved to create some kind of haven – a place where I could relish memories of the past and take delight in the new present. This I did twice. First with my husband in Sussex and later, mainly as a solo operator, in the restoration of a ruined stone barn in Provence. The barn still helps to fend off the toll of advancing years.

I.S.

CONTENTS

I.	From Poland to Siberia	11
II.	Kazakhstan	25
III.	Teheran 1942 – 1944	51
IV.	Uganda 1944 – 1948	65
V.	New life in England	91
VI.	Andrew's childhood	111
VII.	Doozes	127
VIII.	Discovering Provence	137
IX.	Life around Callian	161
X.	Andrew and Pope John Paul II	181
XI.	Farewell Staszek	185

Appendices

1.	Poland in the Second World War	191
2.	Kazakhs and Kazakhstan	201
3.	Uganda	207
4.	UNRRA – UNHCR	225

I. FROM POLAND TO SIBERIA

In the memorable summer of 1939 I was fourteen years old and for the first time spending school holidays away from my parents. I was at a pleasant country estate of my mother's brother Jan, with its vast fields of golden wheat, rye, barley and blue flowered flax swaying in the gentle breeze. The undulating terrain was dotted with small woods of silver birch trees and enclosed on one side by a magnificent forest. A stream was running through meadows covered with sweet scented flowers, and bees, butterflies and larks fluttered above. I was charmed by the scenery and fascinated by country life, with its arduous routine and the various seasonal activities. It was idyllic.

Most exciting were the night expeditions with torches to catch crayfish and the early morning excursions to the forest to pick wild strawberries and search for mushrooms. On Sundays we drove in a smart carriage pulled by two horses to the parish church in Grauzyszki and occasionally returned with the vicar, who sometimes joined us for dinner and a game of cards. Once I waited till midnight, hiding in a hammock under the starfilled sky, hoping to drive the vicar back to Grauzyszki. My offer was met with firm disapproval. I went to bed reminded kindly by my aunt and less kindly by uncle Jan about the proprieties of a young girl's behaviour.

The harvest was the big event in the area and farmers were helping each other by sharing the labour force as well as the newly acquired mechanical harvester. I tried hard to master the sickle. At the conclusion of the harvest a procession of girls with garlands of flowers on their heads and bouquets in their hands came from the fields singing on their way to my uncle's garden for celebrations. The tables were loaded with delicacies and a whole lamb and a calf were roasting over a big fire. The air was saturated with the smell of charcoal, herbs, cakes, home –made lemonade and beer. The roast lamb was my favourite dish, and still is.

An amusing incident occurred one day when I was sent to the so–called "cold–house" for a bucket of cream. It was a sizeable mound of straw and earth in the shape of a flying saucer, nestling in the corner of the kitchen garden. I entered the enclosure through a low door and moved quickly as directed, when suddenly I stumbled waist–deep into a hole filled with freezing water, with big blocks of ice floating on the surface. It was not easy to climb out, and even more uncomfortable to present myself to my aunt, soaking wet and without the cream! But the mystery of the cold drinks and ice–cream was solved!

I loved Gabralowszczyzna and the old timber house with its handsome porch and wide staircase; the farmyard with its barn, dairy, stables, kennels, and the dry store housing rows of cured ham, salami and cheese. The smell of fresh bread baked on maple leaves and the taste of rye blini, served with a thick sauce from lamb or pork ribs, was unforgettable.

I was so preoccupied with outdoor life that I paid little attention to the interior of the house, except for the big central hall with the antlers on the walls. Less elegant but quite impressive were servants' quarters with the dormitory of double bunks, larders and the workshops fully equipped with tools and machinery.

From the front porch to the entrance gate ran an alley lined with linden trees, which I traversed for the very last time at the end of August. I had to return to my family in Grodno, and to school. Uncle Jan took me to Oszmiana, where I said goodbye to other relatives and took a bus to Wilno. I found this beautiful town in great upheaval. Along the streets people were digging trenches and soldiers were marching. Mobilisation had been declared!

I was worried about my return because all trains were reserved for military transports. Somehow I softened the heart of an official and managed to board a train. It was a profoundly new experience for me travelling with grown–ups and hesitatingly taking part in their serious discussions. Suddenly I began to feel like an adult, with my childhood left behind for ever in Gabralowszczyzna.

14

The train arrived in Grodno during a beautiful sunset. The sky was rich in shades of red and purple. I took a horse drawn cab to Jerozolimska street and was met by my parents with relief and joy. The next morning on the first day of September 1939 I was hanging the washing on the line in the garden when suddenly there appeared a squadron of heavy planes, making a thundering noise overhead. Instantly the electrifying sound of sirens warned people to take shelter. The German attack on Poland had begun.

My father was called up to join the army. The atmosphere was tense. Between the siren alarms and the rush to the shelters we spent our time grouped around the radio listening to the news. On September 3rd came the news we were waiting for: England and France had declared war on Germany. This lifted our spirits enormously.

My mother decided to leave our beloved Grodno on the banks of the lovely river Niemen for the safety of a small estate near Smorgonie, named Lopocie. It had been leased for a number of years to Mr Pietraszko, who gave us the use of a room where my mother, myself, and my two younger brothers arranged for our temporary existence. Shortly after, because of its isolation, I was sent to my aunt in Oszmiana to continue my education. My uncle Alexander taught mathematics in the local grammar school.

On the fatal sunny afternoon of September 17th I was walking in the grounds of the hospital in Oszmiana with my uncle Bronislaw, who was director of the hospital, when I was surprised to see him stop suddenly. As though struck by lightening, he turned pale and a nervous twitch appeared at the corner of his mouth. I followed his eyes through the gate of the hospital and saw the column of Russian soldiers, slowly moving in from the East, along the Route Napoleon. I watched the shabbily dressed soldiers and cavalry on thin, small horses, with the feet of the riders almost dragging along the ground. They had made an overnight encampment on the outskirts of the town and were now moving out, leaving a few dead horses behind. This Russian invasion was felt as a tragic blow by my parents' generation, who had lived through the First World War.

For a while life was almost normal, and school continued under the new directorship of a Russian military officer. Not for long though, because a few weeks later I was called into the office and told that I was expelled. "Why?" I asked, shocked by the spectre of ignorance looming in my mind. "There is no room for educating unwanted elements in communist society" I was told. "You have no right to do this" I cried, "education is like air and water, free for all, especially in the communist system!" I was ashamed at being unable to control the tears in my eyes. I was then pushed out of the room.

I continued living with my aunt because we heard that my father had been arrested and imprisoned in Oszmiana. We tried to pass him a parcel of warm clothes; the winter of 1939 was extremely severe. One fearfully cold day I was waiting with many others at the prison gate to hand my parcel to the guards, but the gates remained closed. Waiting so long I lost all feeling in my hands and feet as the temperature was dropping to -18°C. Suddenly the gate opened to let a car out. The crowd pushed forward and being at the front I skidded, loosing my grip on the bundle which rolled past the closing gate. It was the only one to pass the gate that day. Later we heard that it had been delivered.

My frost bitten fingers bothered me for a long time. Just before Christmas I returned to Lopocie. Inactivity tended to deepen my depression, so I started exploring my surroundings, made new friends in the nearest village and listened to the stories of the peasants. Some were very sad and troubled my conscience. They did not enhance my idealised vision of Poland, but it stimulated a great sympathy for these simple people whose life was hard.

One man told me about a visit of the sequestrate, entering his house taking, among other things, the only pillow from under the head of his dying mother, because he could not pay his taxes. A family of seven was living together with their animals in one cottage, the five children sharing a pair of shoes, going to school in turns. One man described the fire in a neighbouring manor. The villagers gathered to look and to help, and then the lord appeared with a tray, demanding that everyone contribute money for the restoration. "What a monster", I thought.

The girls were chatting about their Sunday walks to church, carrying their shoes on a stick over their shoulder, putting them only on at the entrance to the church. But aside from the sad experiences, there were also happy moments of village social life. I was invited to village homes to join in singing and dancing. I danced the polka in their fashion, with spread out elbows and vigorous stamping of the feet. I also shared their food, eating from the large common dish with a wooden spoon.

I watched the young men, some of them very handsome, with blond hair and blue eyes. The ones with military service behind them had easy manners and were not shy talking. Their mothers were proud of them, as they returned home with a tooth brush, an implement generally not to be found in the village. I began to imagine that if the situation would not change I should marry one of them in a few years' time and work as unremittingly as they but perhaps with the help of modern machinery sent by wealthy American cousins.

My brothers were spending their time in their own male way. One day they came home behaving unbecomingly. They were drunk! Apparently when watching the men making vodka in the forest they were given some of the first drops to drink, much to the amusement of their hosts.

During the winter we noticed that the boots of the boys were leaking, so I set out with my mother to a shoemaker in a distant village with a sack of worn–out shoes. The shoemaker examined them carefully, scratched his head and said: "I can't repair these, I do not have the leather to fill the holes", pointing to the cut–out pattern of the sandals. So we left the cobbler with four pairs of wooden clogs and a can of paraffin from the village shop. The four–kilometre walk through the snow–covered fields and the dense pine forest, so pleasant in the morning, had changed into a spooky trek after sunset. We walked with the can and the sack of clogs suspended from a stick between us. It was getting cold and the snow was becoming crunchy under our feet. In the darkness we noticed two bright spots moving in parallel behind the nearest trees. It was a wolf! I was petrified. The terrible stories told about encounters with wolves welled up in my mind, but my mother calmed me down. She picked up a broken branch lying in the snow and poured some paraffin onto it, and lit it. We ran madly from the woods into the open.

We spend the next day getting used to our clogs–and that required some practice. When we got used to them we had great fun cracking frozen snow crust, for in the second–half of February the midday sun melted the surface of the deep snow, and then the night frost formed a brittle crust of ice.

The general situation under Russian occupation was going from bad to worse. The withdrawal of Polish currency from circulation was critical. My mother tried hard to give variety to our diet, which was based on potatoes, carrots and beetroots in addition to the milk from our cow, and the bread made from the sack of flour we bought on our arrival to Lopocie. I learnt how to milk the cow, and soon learned how to stop the milk running up my sleeves.

Rumours about forthcoming deportations to Siberia began to circulate and the atmosphere became ever more depressing. At the beginning of March, my mother decided to go to her family in Oszmiana to ask for help. One night, while she was away, a loud banging on the door woke up the whole household. A few minutes later the door to our room opened and two armed Russian soldiers entered with an order: "Gather up your belongings and be ready to leave in one hour!" They lit a lamp and looked at our sleepy and terrified faces, disregarding the absence of our mother and not even asking about her. One dashed to the cupboard full of papers and books, and began to investigate them, whilst the other harried me to get dressed and to stop the boys from crying. They were really miserable, unaware of the stark reality of the situation. They just called "Mamma! Mamma!"

I was in shock and did not know how to console them; they were crying helplessly. Janusz was just twelve and Tadzik nine. The soldiers urged us to start packing and told us to take warm clothes for the long journey. We had nothing really suitable, just our school coats. The boys boots were at the cobbler. I looked enviously at Mr Pietraszko's sheepskin coat hanging in the hall, but did not dare to ask him for it. He showed no understanding of our plight.

Gradually my panic subsided and a feeling of responsibility took over. I helped the boys get ready, packed the suitcases, leaving all mother's clothes in the wardrobe, and tied up a bundle of bedding in a blanket. I then looked around anxiously for a bag of salt, recollecting somebody saying it was vital for human existence. The watching soldiers questioned my concern and on hearing my explanation burst into hearty laughter. "Don't worry. We have plenty of salt in Russia, but we don't have anything to put it on". A soldier, finding nothing suspicious among our papers, and no money at all, gave me a ten rouble note: "you can't go on a long journey like this with no money", he said. I was surprised by his unexpected generosity and touched by this evidence of the Russian soul.

They made a list of confiscated items on a scrappy piece of paper in pencil and handed it to me "for your record". By the porch a big horse–driven cart was waiting for us and we piled into it with our bundles. I had time to run back to our room for more rugs and newspapers to wrap our feet and also grabbed some plates and kitchenware. Dawn was breaking as we left Lopocie. The Pietraszkos were in tears, making the sign of cross over our heads.

On our way to the railway station in Soly we passed through two villages. They must have been forewarned because people were standing in front of their houses in the dim early morning light waving to us, giving us their blessings, even throwing loaves of bread into the cart. It made me feel very, very sad.

Suddenly we saw a horseman in the distance, galloping towards us through the field of melting snow. We recognised Antoni, the young Pietraszko. He put a sack of part–repaired shoes in the cart; he had brought them from the cobbler. We thanked him warmly for his thoughtfulness and I felt better.

Waiting at the station was a long goods–train, almost fully packed with people. We were pushed into the wagon with about half a dozen other families. People were sitting beside mounds of luggage, big cases and chests, there was even a sowing machine. Compared with the others, our luggage was miniscule. By now the three of us were completely dispirited. We felt lost without our mother. We were completely indifferent to our new companions who sized us up, not showing any interest or affection towards us. The train remained stationary during the night with its doors locked.

In the morning there was a violent agitation outside, then the door opened, and it was like a dream: our mother was standing on a cart by the door waving her umbrella, crying and shouting with emotion. She looked glorious! After this ecstatic outburst she told us about her dramatic ordeal: "In Oszmiana I heard about the deportations so I immediately hurried back to Lopocie. I found the room empty except for my umbrella standing in the corner of the wardrobe. I grasped it and took a few pieces of hidden silver and an old samovar. I implored the coachman to hurry to Soly. On the way, villagers told me about you being taken the previous night. I filled the samovar with vodka and took a sip now and then for encouragement and arrived at the station in a boisterous mood. I was so pleased to find the train still there. I was prepared to follow even to Vladivostok. Standing on the cart which was moving along the length of the train I banged my umbrella on the door of each wagon and demanded the guard to open it for my inspection. That was my last twenty four hours." She smiled, embracing us warmly. What a wonderful mother!

Shortly after we heard the metallic rattle of the wheels and the train began to pull out. Each wagon was locked from outside, with an armed soldier standing on a small platform projecting out at one end. Inside there was a wide wooden deck and a tiny barred window high up in the corner. The other occupants were the families of Polish officers and policeman, farmers, and, to my surprise, a game–keeper's wife with six children between three and eleven years old, all dressed in heavy linen outfits. We made arrangements for the night, half of us sleeping on the floor, and the rest on the deck. I settled close to the window so as to see and get more air. Fortunately, my mother was warmly dressed, the lack of her belongings seemed not to worry her. I did however feel troubled at leaving so much behind in the village.

The train was moving slowly across the plains of Belarus with occasional stops at small stations, where we were allowed to get a bucket of boiling water from huge barrels standing on the platform. Permanent fires were burning beneath them. At that time this was general practice in Russia. We called them "The Big Samovars".

Problems associated with "the call of nature" were solved when the train stopped once a day in a completely isolated locality. The "passengers" were urged to crawl under it. The only man in our wagon, Mr Sturlis, had an axe and made a hole in the floor for emergencies. Occasionally we were permitted to walk for a few minutes along the train to meet old friends or make new ones. I made no new acquaintances, but friendships began to develop between the occupants of our carriage. Children were playing in a corner and women were exchanging their life stories and speculating on the future. As often as possible I tried to get to the window to see the outside world and whatever we were leaving behind. From time to time the train would pass a village still buried in snow with streaks of smoke rising from the chimneys. Quite often people ran along the train, begging for bread.

I recorded all my experiences in a diary, writing in the dim light of a paraffin lantern. Near Moscow we passed a river, so big that it looked like a lake. It was beautiful sight, with a multitude of floating chunks of ice. Later, the landscape changed, becoming hilly with occasional woods. We climbed slowly towards the Urals. We crossed the mountains during the night under the full moon, and although the window bars were freezing my fingers, I was hypnotised by the beauty of the mountains. It was completely new experience and I was entranced by the snowy ridges glittering like diamonds, the mountain peaks became towers of imaginary castles perched above dark gorges. The tall snow–laden pines swayed gently in the breeze. The air was sharp and pure. It was magic.

At some distance east of the Urals, our train left the Trans –Siberian railway line of Pietropavlovsk, from where it went in a southerly direction. In the morning mist, it stopped at Kokchetav where we were ordered to transfer into waiting lorries. It was drizzling and the snow was beginning to melt on the half–frozen ground. We were now at the end of April and the smell of spring was already in the air.

II. KAZAKHSTAN 1940–1942

We drove through the outskirts of Kokchetav, a town of small wooden houses with pitched roofs. The smoke rising from the chimneys looked friendly and inviting. The cobbled streets gave way to a vast plain. On the horizon the endless steppe merged with the sky. The first impression of its scale and vast emptiness was depressing. There was nothing to rest one's eye on. The bad weather robbed the landscape of any charm. The patches of snow scattered over the ground looked grey and dull.

We passed through a settlement, which broke the monotony. In a few more hours we reached our destination: Kolkhoz Zoldubay.

The lorries stopped outside the village and we climbed down from the lorries onto the melting snow. Soon after our cold and miserable looking group was surrounded by strange looking men, who were to be our hosts. They looked Asiatic with high cheekbones, slanted eyes, thin beards, and moustaches hanging down each side of rather thin lips. They were of impressive posture wearing well cut fur coats, high leather boots reaching above the knees and enormous caps. They were the Kazakhs. The NKVD officer, our guardian, so to speak, made a short speech telling us that our future would be in Zoldubay with the Kazakhs. Then he departed with the lorries.

The men looked us over for a while and after some discussion between themselves, families were approached and given the sign to follow. We were approached by a middle aged, energetic looking man who introduced himself as Dziesiumbay, who then led us to his saray, the enclosure where he had his dwelling. His wife, Kubayla, was waiting for us and invited us into their house. She was a small, likeable woman with a nice smile and big questioning eyes. She wore a colourful jerkin over many layers of fabrics and a white bonnet that looked rather like a helmet.

Entering their house was like stepping back into prehistoric times. It was located in the corner of a large enclosed yard – saray – and we entered through a small door. It was a square shaped dwelling of about 20 meters square divided into two parts. The part near the entrance had a floor of beaten earth and a narrow fireplace with a chimney rising to the ceiling and an opening for cooking at floor level. Rough wooden planks covered the other half concealing a big hole in the centre, which served as a store.

Walls of the house were more than half a metre thick, built in an ancient way of two rows of interwoven wattle, about two metres high. The void was filled with a mixture of earth and cow dung. The roof was constructed in similar manner. A small window faced the door. The walls and ceiling were roughly plastered with clay and chalk. There not many furnishings. A pile of furs on the plank floor, a small stool by the stove and some clothes hanging by the door.

The first night spent in the Dziesiumbay's house was certainly unusual and even amusing, as we were making arrangements for six people to sleep on the floor. The Kazakhs stretched out on their thick soft furs, and we braved the night with our thin blankets which were no obstacle to the splinters. Our covers were inadequate, nevertheless the small space soon warmed up with our breathing and we slept soundly, even though our host snored enthusiastically!

In the morning Kubayla gave us tea in nicely painted wooden bowls, with a piece of flat bread called lepioshki, baked in the hot ashes of her stove. Then we left to explore the surroundings. In the other corner of the saray stood Dziesiumbay's impressive new house. Built of pine logs, it was nearing completion and they were planning to move in shortly .Other parts of the yard were occupied by stacks of hay and straw, a cart, a horse and a few chickens.

Till recently, the Kazakhs led a nomadic life, moving across the steppes with their big tents called yurts. The communist system changed all that and forced them to settle down in organised communities, the kolkhozes. At Zoldubay these were built along the wide main road as a row of fenced yards – the sarays. They contained a simple dwelling and provision for animals. Many Kazakhs kept their yurts in the middle of the yard, using it only for special occasions.

There were about fifty households along the road which sloped towards the marshes. Towards the other end was a large dairy. Some Kazakhs, including Dziesiumbay, began to build more substantial houses. The kolkhoz was surrounded by the steppe, the nearer part by now transformed into cultivated fields. On the horizon one could see a black line of forest, closer to the village were some shrubs and a lovely grove of silver birch trees.

There was no sign of a well so we asked about it and were shown the marches where a little stream of brown water trickled through the soggy ground, thickly overgrown with weeds. Water had to stand for a long time in various large vessels, then filtered, boiled and strained before our mother allowed us to drink it. We were already thinking of the next winter when we could have pure water from the melted snow. Luckily there were cows in the kolkhoz and we were entitled to a ration of milk.

Meeting up with the other members of our group we chatted about how and when we would adapt to the new reality. Somehow, with the weather improving and Kazakhs treating us with sympathy, our morale improved and we began arranging our new life in Zoldubay. Two momentous events happened. First, mother's sister sent a parcel with clothes and some money. Second, Dziesiumbay moved into his new house and we bought his old one.

Immediately we began adapting it to our needs and I made a list of priorities:1 – beds, 2 – table and stools, 3 – stove. My mother found the Kazakh stove most unsuitable and engaged two men to demolish it and build one in Russian style which facilitated cooking and baking at elbow level instead of on the floor . It was an impressive structure built with sun dried mud bricks. It took up a lot of room but was effective for cooking and bread baking. The warm space between the top and the roof would melt the snow in winter and so kept the house beautifully warm. Mama was satisfied.

I worked on the beds but the great problem was our lack of tools. Dziesiumbay lent us his axe and his saw, but he had no nails and no string. So came our first improvisation. With my brothers I went to the woods and we collected a few fallen, well seasoned trees. We cut twelve legs for three beds: one for mama, one for me and one for the boys. Laboriously with a knife and the axe we made grooves at one end of the legs to insert members of the frame. We tied them together with flexible birch twigs and stabilized the frame with another line of branches below and fixed diagonal pieces. For the mattresses we obtained some big burlap sacks from the kolkhoz and filled them with dry grass from the steppe. Fortunately I brought from Lopocie some needles and cotton, so the sacks were sown strongly. The sensation of stretching on the bed was sleep inducing, like lying on a rocking boat. The table was made in the same ad hoc fashion, with a top formed of strong planks. A set of nicely trimmed logs was a good solution for the seating. We finished the improvements by giving the walls a white wash with chalk we dug out from the steppe. Mama baked loaves of bread in her new stove and sometimes we ate the flat lepioshki. We were really pleased with our improvisations. The main problem apart from drinking water was the lack of sanitation: no latrines, neither private nor communal. I noticed Kazakhs disappearing each morning behind their sarays with a kettle of water and returning with a smile and an empty kettle. What an excellent idea, I thought.

However, we could not take to their way of spring cleaning. With the first sign of warm sunshine they would emerge from their houses to settle comfortably at the foot of the walls. The sight was spectacular. The men would divest themselves of their clothes from the waist up one by one. Then they stretched their shirts by the seams with their hands and with their teeth went from one end to the other with the noise of a light machine gun…tra ta ta…This was their way of killing lice. After repeating the operation for each seam they shook the skirt vigorously and put it back on. Women were searching each other's heads for vermin, killing them with their finger nails. We desperately tried to keep our bodies clean, not at all easy without soap. The only way was to rub aggressively with a cloth, rinsed frequently. I had my long hair made into plaits down to my waist and I used to clean them with beaten egg.

The most difficult thing was washing our clothes. It was done at a little stream in the marshes, where we made a small pool and used sand to rub the dirty clothes before rinsing them in the pool. How long would our fabrics last with this regime?

We suffered greatly from a lack of vegetables. The Kazakh diet consisted mainly of bread, cow's milk, eggs and occasional piece of boiled horse meat. In the kolkhoz there was no vegetable garden and no flowers or shrubs. A few onions we received in a parcel from Oszmiana we planted on the roof but they were dug up secretly during the night and the next morning Dzie-siumbay said gravely: "Victoria, we love you and you can live with us peacefully, but we can't tolerate any such innovations, it is against our religion".

From then on we were restricted to what nature offered and as long as summer lasted we enjoyed stinging nettles, dandelion, sorrel, some shoots from trees as well certain ground roots, some of which we dried for the coming winter. We were supposed to work, but there was very little to do because the Kazakhs were not trained in agriculture. They were still dreaming of returning to their nomadic life. They were cherishing their precious rifles. Now, much of their time was spent sitting on the floor with crossed legs or lying on their furs smoking a pipe, chatting, and often spitting, which apparently was a sign of appreciation and approval.

In the spring we were sent on our first assignment – to plant potatoes. While distributing them in a deep ditch dug in the ground, I stopped suddenly on hearing a familiar phrase, which I remembered from Lopocie. Dropping the basket I ran to my mother, calling with excitement that some Kazakhs spoke Polish. When I repeated the phrase my mother laughed and explained that it was a dreadful Russian swear word, unfortunately still used by the peasants of north–east Poland.

They were Muslims greeting everybody with "salam aleykum". The communist system was still alien to them and Stalin was considered an enemy because he deprived them of their sacred pilgrimages to Mecca. Dziesiumbay showed us proudly his varnished rifles and skins of deer, wolves and hares. He spoke Russian quite well, but to Kubayla, we communicated with the help of signs and smiles.

When the birth of their child was imminent they asked my mother to be midwife and godmother of the baby. Their six previously born children had all died in their first year, so now they were putting all their hope in Victoria, who accepted the honour. Poor Kubayla gave birth in the traditional manner, suspended from the beam in accordance with their custom, in vertical position. It was a fine baby boy and a few days later there was a great celebration in the saray. I was amazed at the variety of milk products. There were sweets of different shapes and sizes, chewy balls and the delicious ayran. A big leather bag full of mare's milk, known as kumys, circulated among the numerous relatives and Victoria was treated reverentially.

The role of a midwife was very important to the Kazakhs and my mother by custom was entitled to a substantial reward. However, she did not accept anything. She simply asked the chairman "predsiedatel" of the kolkhoz, a brother of Dziesiumbay, to loan her a cart in which, with some other women, she would go to a distant Russian kolkhoz for some flour, potatoes and cabbages in exchange for some items of our clothing. Our dear mother was an incredibly resourceful person.

During the summer we helped harvest the magnificent wheat in fields some distance from the village and at the end every worker was paid with a set amount of grain. When my turn came Dziesiumbay, who was in charge of weighting, threw onto my shoulder an enormous sack of wheat and I collapsed on the ground. It must have been over sixty kilos, twice what other women received. This happened in the fields a few kilometres from the kolkhoz. I struggled painfully to my feet and slowly dragged the sack along. It was getting late and my companions had disappeared in the darkness. I rested a while at the roadside then continued at a snail's pace, but of course I could not leave the sack. Finally, my brothers arrived, sent by my anxious mother, and together we brought the bounty home. It provided us with food for weeks, but the grinding of the corn presented a serious problem. Mama persuaded Dziesiumbay to lend us his old grinder, which consisted of two grooved millstones. About 40 cm in diameter. A handful of grain was thrown through a hole in the upper stone and was ground by persistent turning. The crushed grain was put through several sieves to separate parts for different uses: fine flour for making pasta and bread, the rough cast – so called kasha – for grainy dishes, lastly the pearl barley. It was great fun.

One day towards the end of October, Dziesiumbay burst in crying "Victoria, help us". The NKVD had arrived and started searching the houses at the top of the village. He pulled out his horse and cart, loaded it with sacks of grain and asked Victoria to help him drive to the steppes to hide the stuff. While they were away I was helping Kubayla bring sacks of wheat from their house to ours to hide them in the hole under the floor . We also brought the rifles and put them under my mother's mattress. We were working at such a pitch that for a few days afterwards my hands were so stiff I couldn't move my fingers at all.

The return of Victoria and Dziesiumbay coincided with the arrival of the officers who went through everything in the saray, poking their rifles into the stacks of hay before entering Dzie-siumbay's house and turning it completely upside down. Frustrated; they came to our little home with some arrogance, but changed their manner when my mother addressed them in fluent Russian. She spent some time during the revolution in Jaroslav on the Volga, where she encountered the Bolsheviks and got to know their "soft spots". The searches became more polite and left our things alone. One looked with interest at our few books and picked one up. I shuddered. It was "Wielki Cham" {The Great Yoke}, which I brought from Lopocie .It is about the wrongs of the Russian Revolution. The officer tried to read: and he smiled triumphantly: "The Great Chan"! I congratulated him on his knowledge of the Latin alphabet and they left, saluting mother with respect.

Finally they left Zoldubay with a lorry full of arrested Kazakhs and all the grain they had found. This was punishment for not delivering to the government the required quota of grain. The village was full of sadness. Then, to my mother's despair, the snow came. Hiding the sacks in such a hurry, no marks or signs were made and she searched in vain for days. Luckily Kubayla had enough grain under our floor to last her and her nearest family through winter.

Then came the news of the arrival of a young teacher, Ludmila, and the opening of a village school. All children were called to attend, me included, and all ages assembled to take lessons together. It gave me the opportunity to improve my knowledge of Russian and to read the poetry of Pushkin and Turgenev which I borrowed from Ludmila who became my great friend. At last it was possible to read in the evening thanks to supply of paraffin to the village shop which was before permanently empty. It was sold at one litre per queuing person but with no register, so we returned to the shop again and again until all the cans and bottles in the house were full. Once that winter was a delivery of small sweets like little raspberries, they were much appreciated. The first winter passed with no hitches or serious illnesses.

In the spring our men returned from arrest and the seasonal routine of the kolkhoz started with the cleaning out of the barns and the dairy. Ankle deep in manure, we loaded the stuff onto carts to spread it later over the fields. I found my wooden clogs very useful for this work as they were easy to clean. During the hot summer of 1941 we worked in distant fields which we reached by horse or oxen. On one occasion, riding an ox along the marshes, the beast stopped stubbornly in a swamp enjoying the cooling sensation. It ignored my crying and kicks and I was smothered with flies and bitten by mosquitoes.

My brother Tadzik was thrown by the horse and broke his leg. We were panic–stricken. But, the senior Kazakh, skilfully applied a dressing of some herbs between two boards firmly tied round the leg, and sent Tadzik home. A few weeks later after frequent changes of moss and weeds, Tadzik's leg recovered.

Through mother's sister in Oszmiana we learned that uncle Bronislaw's wife had also been deported with her two daughters to Kazakhstan and was living in a kolkhoz near Kokczetav. I decided to find them and got a lift to town from an agricultural engineer who was in Zoldubay researching the water situation in the area. It was a very pleasant ride in a smart two wheel cart, but most interesting was what I heard on the way. The engineer was a dedicated communist who told me all sorts of stories glorifying the Party. I have forgotten them except the rendering of his dream: "You will witness that life in communist Russia will soon rise to the zenith of perfection. People will be working only three days a week and for the remaining time they will be resting on a pile of straw, from floor to window sill deep, and they will be eating slice after slice of lard". {"salo salem zakusojet"}. I could not believe my ears. And he was an educated man.

In the middle of July we heard, well after the catastrophic event, that the war had broken out between Germany and Russia. At the beginning it did not affect us except that the visits of the NKVD became less frequent. Soon letters and parcels no longer came from Poland. My aunt moved to Kokchetav and found work in a hospital. A group of Polish women from our kolkhoz went to the Kokchetav market. I joined them carrying our last bundle of net curtains rolled in a beautiful red shawl belonging to my grandmother. Half way there we were overtaken by a Russian kolkhoznik who offered to carry our luggage on his cart. Later, I caught up with the cart and looked for my bundle. "What bundle? I haven't seen any bundle", said the man with a curse. It was a great shock. I found my aunt and cried on her shoulder.

I could not contemplate returning home to mother with this news so I decided to find some work. Good aunt Janina took me in and I shared a bed with my younger cousin Busia. A few days later I got work at the town garden and received my ration card entitling me to buy bread and sugar, which was sold in lumps that resembled big stones. Because of the acute shortage of everything, sugar was special and there was popular joke about four ways of drinking tea with sugar: First, putting apiece of sugar into a cup of tea "v prikusku". Secondly, licking a cube of sugar suspended on a string and sipping the tea "v prilizku", thirdly, looking only at the cube of sugar "v prigladku", and fourthly, thinking about sugar "v pridumku".

I worked for a week, cheerfully carrying buckets and watering the miserable looking plants. On receiving my first week's pay I was told by the official that it was a waste of human resources when the country was at war, and he dismissed me.

It was too early to return to Zoldubay to eat my mother's bread, so I began to look for another job and heard of a permanent position in the brick factory outside town. I hurried there full of expectations in spite of my aunt's disapproval. The building was a big brick – built barn with hundreds of workers sleeping there between shifts. I was accepted and given three boards for a bed and told to find a place for it. I wondered a long time through the designated sleeping areas before I found a tiny place between sleepers in the huge dormitory.

My ten hours shift started at midday. The production area was primitive. No machinery was evident because everything was done by hand. I had to carry the unbaked bricks to the kiln. They were shoved onto my outstretched arms by two men. Four bricks were manageable but with six I was staggering. Finishing close to midnight, I dropped half dead on my boards, shivering with cold and unable to sleep because I had no blankets.

Next morning I asked to be put on the night shift. I was afraid I could not survive another night, like the last one. It was agreed and I worked through the nights, resting at my aunt's place during the day. At the end of a terrible week with a breakfast of boiled barley with a drop of oil on top and a piece of bread of the consistency and colour of wet brick, I collected my week's pay. In the factory shop I bought a pair of sandals made of a piece of tractor tyre with string to tie it round my ankles. I decided to run away from the factory to end this nightmare.

It was the end of September, weather was changing and the morning was grey with drizzling rain. The road to town was deserted except for three figures kneeling in the mud in front of a dilapidated Russian church near the road. Intrigued, I approached them and asked: "What are you doing here in this atrocious weather?" "We are praying to God for the Germans to come soon because we can't go on like this any longer" was the answer. They were surprised to see me on such a deserted road and I had to tell them of my escape. I left them with a message for my aunt and continued to Zoldubay. It was a difficult walk in the rain and deep mud. It was more than eight hours before I kissed my mother. She looked at me with pity , pointing at my muddy feet with the string around my ankles. I could not remember where and when I parted company with my new sandals.

During my absence my dear brave mother had lengthy talk with the seniors of the kolkhoz and convinced them of the need for a proper well and finally, digging was to go ahead. During the autumn rains our roof sprang several leaks and we had to take shelter under the beds. When the weather improved a little we collected the round, flat slabs of cow dung on the steppes, storing them in the saray as fuel for the winter. Some Polish families decided to apply for permission to leave Zoldubay to work on an extension of the railway from Kokchetav to Karaganda.

The second winter began to look very grim. No more parcels and nothing left to exchange. More and more people fell ill with the flu and there was no medicine. My mother was struck down by a high fever. She remembered a remedy practiced by country folk: "banki". Tiny, specially shaped glasses were heated and applied quickly to the back. This required swift, skilful heating of the glass done by inserting momentarily a burning cotton wad, immersed in spirit. The hot banki were quickly applied to the skin and they became attached to the back. Since we had neither banki, cotton or spirit I gathered all the smallest glass jars I could find, stuffed them with burning pieces of paper – some were still burning in the glass on my mother's back. But it worked. After removing them ten minutes later with a whisper–like noise, my mother's back was covered with brown circles. She soon got better. I began to make the rounds to the houses of the sick, perfecting my skill. The Kazakhs were impressed and asked me to treat them as well, calling me: Jerka Wracz (doctor). It was a problem to treat them, because they were pointing to painful parts of their bodies where the banki would not adhere: elbows, knees and shoulder blades. They did not understand my explanations so I had to treat them, hoping for the best by applying the glasses on the nearest fleshy parts.

In response, on our doorstep we found boxes of eggs, butter and even meat. I was also invited to join them at a ceremonial meal in their Yurt in the middle of a saray. We sat on the ground covered with colourful rugs and furs around the fire with a big pot of simmering food hanging over it .Before the meal a copper bowl and a kettle of water were passed around for washing hands. Then the lady of the house dished out the food with a wooden ladle into very nice wooden bowls and passed them to the guests. It was stewed horse meat in a thick sauce with a kind of pasta. We ate with our fingers , using the round bread. After the meal, the kettle and the bowl circulated again for rinsing hands, then tea was served in small painted bowls. Men were drinking kumys, a potent fermented mare's milk. While seated, they were turning backwards, spitting to their heart's content.

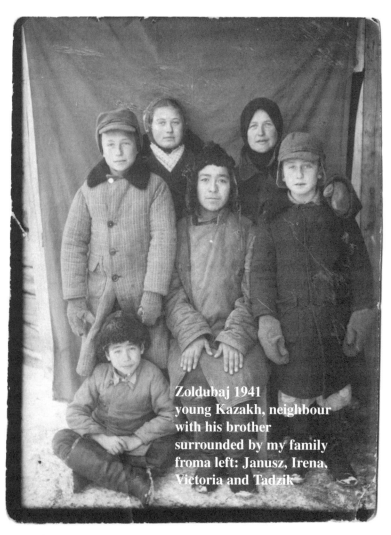

Zoldubaj 1941
young Kazakh, neighbour
with his brother
surrounded by my family
froma left: Janusz, Irena,
Victoria and Tadzik

After the spell of colds and flu was over, we developed a
strange sensation in our limbs and our teeth loosened. This happened only to the newcomers, not to the Kazakhs. Each day we
had greater difficulty in grinding the corn until we could scarcely
turn the stone at all. We had to be satisfied with eating boiled
wheat instead of bread. Nor could we lift the buckets of water

from the newly dug well to carry home. By some chance we came across a copy of a Red Cross letter with underlined phrases referring to scurvy. The strong advice was to collect pine needles and consume as many as possible in any form: chew them raw, make salad or use them for infusion. Pine needles contain highly concentrated vitamin C. Straight away my brothers and I scrambled through the deep snow to the nearby birch woods, where there were some pines. We chewed and chewed the needles and filled our pockets with them for our mama. The next time we went with friends and with baskets. The result was absolutely miraculous within a few weeks the change was most noticeable and soon our legs regained their normal movement and our teeth stopped behaving like piano keys. Mother baked a ceremonial loaf of bread after we resumed grinding the first few cups of grain.

One day near Christmas 1941, we heard great commotion outside our house. In the thickly falling snow we saw a man looking like a father Christmas, on the sledge. At that moment Dziesiumbay walked in shouting "Victoria, your husband". A minute later, a snow–covered figure entered, surrounded by Kazakhs. It was my father. Overwhelmed with emotion we ran to him for embraces and kisses, bombarding him with questions.

How? Why? When? He was an intriguing figure in an unfamiliar military uniform with the insignia of a Polish officer and a great scar above his right eye. After he was comfortably installed came his incredible story. Soon after the German attack on Russia in July 1941, the Polish government in exile in London re–established relations with Russia, changing the previous status of enemy to that of an ally. General Sikorski, our Prime Minister, went to Moscow and secured from Stalin amnesty for all prisoners of war and organised the formation of a Polish army in Russia with General Anders as commander. When the news reached him, our father was recovering from a near–fatal accident in the taiga of northern Siberia. While cutting timber on swampy ground a tree fell on him almost crushing his head. He was to be left for dead, but the other prisoners protested vigorously and permission was given for one of them, a surgeon, to carry out an operation. Father recovered and regained his vision, but one eyelid remained rigid and he could never close it. He joined the Polish army and arrived at its headquarters in Buzuluk where all the soldiers were issued with British uniforms. According to rumour, General Sikorski, during his visit to Moscow, said to Stalin: "You have a lot of problems with your own army. So let our soldiers, your starving ex– prisoners, be fed and dressed by the other allies. Let the British do it.". Father immediately sought out his family, and found us in Zoldubay.

The week that followed was wonderful, but then came time for him to say goodbye. He wanted to take us with him, but because of severe winter and mother's poor health he decided to postpone it till spring.

Soon after, a group of German settlers whose ancestors came to Russia at the time of Catherine II at the end of 18th century, were deported from the Volga region and brought to Zoldubay to be housed with Kazakhs. I was excited by the new arrivals and the next day went to meet a family of two women and a girl. I knocked on the door and entered their room. The girl jumped and exclaimed: "I know you, I saw you in my dream during our journey, sitting by the road on a stone and watching us passing in a cart. You were dressed as you are now", she added. It was inexplicable, because there wasn't a road with the stone near our village, and they came in a lorry not a cart. Anyhow, we became good friends and I visited them often, trying to learn a little German.

Towards the spring many of my compatriots became seriously ill and "banki" gave no result. Mrs. Rogowska, a mother of four, was in a critical condition. My mother persuaded the seniors of kolkhoz to take her on a sledge to the hospital in

Kokchetav. I went with her and recently recovered son Ryszard. It was a nightmarish ride through a storm. The snow was blinding the horses and the wind penetrated our clothes. Poor Mrs. Rogowska passed into a coma and by the time we arrived at the hospital, she was dead. The nurses took her body, the coachman went with Ryszards to his friends for the night and I went to my aunt.

Next morning ten years old Ryszard met me tearfully at the hospital and we asked to see the body. The mortuary, situated in a corner of hospital grounds, was full of stiff, grey bodies, reminding me of trunks of trees with stretched out branches. I noticed in the middle of a heap of bodies the red dressing gown of Mrs. Rogowska. Glancing at the desperate face of her young son standing in the doorway, I decided to recover the garment and give it to him, not simply for sentimental reason but with its potential for bread in mind. As though possessed by the devil I started to heave the frozen bodies aside, working with my bare hands through the pile of corpses until I reached the satin gown. Later that day we organised the burial and found a carpenter who undertook to make a coffin in twenty four hours. For the funeral it was necessary to obtain permission from the local police. I got a great shock when I was told that Mrs. Rogowska had died of typhoid. She had already been buried anonymously in a common grave and a sanitary patrol was on the way to Zoldubay, where a quarantine would be imposed.

Hearing this alarming news, I decided to leave Kokchetav immediately, since I did not want to endanger my cousin, whose bed I was sharing. Ryszard was under the care of his friend in town, so I headed home alone. It was a warm sunny day and walking in the heavy spring snow was very tiring, especially with the new knee–high felt boots on my feet. I gladly accepted a lift from two Russians going my way on a cart full of straw. I have no recollection of that ride, and learned later that I became delirious, frequently falling from the cart into the snow, picked up and put back on the straw. Finding the road through Zoldubay barred , the men dropped me by the barrier and went off on the detour.

By the time I was found and taken home I had regained consciousness an was surprised to find my mother in bed. A young woman doctor was bent over her with a stethoscope. Holding mother's little gold cross on a chain in her hand, she said "Where is this God of yours? Why is He not helping you, so that you rely on me, a communist?"

The next day both of us were packed onto a sledge and taken to a small hospital in a distant Russian kolkhoz because no more beds were available at Kokchetav. My mother was in a critical condition, but she was saved by a gentle, elderly doctor from the Volga settlers. I recovered first, lamenting the loss of my waist–long blond braids which I saw being thrown into a furnace in the bathroom, while the nurse was helping me into a hot bath. I was worried about my brothers, but on return to Zoldubay I found them safe and sound, although for three weeks they had a very bad time. It was very distressing to learn that Mrs. Bozenska had died in Kokchetav hospital, leaving two daughters. The only family not infected by typhoid fever was Mrs. Wolkowa and her six children. They were an exceptional family. Constantly in the same linen outfits, they nevertheless were always clean and proper. Every evening they knelt with their mother to pray and sing the litany. They never complained. Our mother joined us a few weeks later and slowly regained her health and strength.

Shortly after these terrible experiences I made a trip to Kokchetav and discovered a newly established Polish refugee centre which was distributing indispensible articles to Poles in need. There were: soap, sugar, rice, tea, and various preserves. I became the official delegate from our kolkhoz and made regular journeys to town, bringing back each time a sack of these essentials to share with each family. I was also given a pair of smart brown leather shoes to protect me on the long journey, which I normally made barefoot. The distance of forty kilometres took me roughly eight hours, it was a pleasant jogging through the vast steppe with its wide horizon. There were a few small groups of pine trees on the way, so I helped myself to pine needles, chewing them and singing along the way until I reached a biggish lake on the outskirts of Kokchetav. I plunged into its refreshing water. On one occasion, floating on my back, I heard fisherman shouting in a frightened voice: "A dead body!". When I raised my head he took me for a ghost and nearly fell off his boat.

Once my aunt allowed me to bring my cousin Busia back to spend a week with us. This time the walk took longer. We had to deal with viper which was curled up in the middle of our path. We were receiving letters and documents from our father right through winter and spring, but the illnesses meant we could not attempt the journey to join him in Buzuluk, or later in Jangijul. I resumed visits to the NKVD in Kokchetav to obtain permission for the train journey from Kazakhstan. The delays persisted until we received news that my father had been transferred to the Middle East. In August my aunt left Kokchetav to join her husband Bronislaw, who was now representing my father in an attempt to get us out.

We packed our belongings and moved to town, taking over our aunt's little flat and depositing our luggage at the railway station. Before leaving Zoldubay I begged Mrs.Wolkowa to allow her youngest daughter come with us, but she stubbornly refused. The weeks in town were busy with frequent visits to the police and to the station to check that our luggage was still there.

One day I witnessed an astonishing scene. Beside long passenger train stationary on the line, hundreds of people were erecting provisional shelters with boxes, boards and canvas.

They were evacuees from Stalingrad. I noticed some elegant women with painted finger nails, hats and make up who were removing their belongings from the train and arranging them in the improvised shelters. I approached them, hungry for news and heard distressing stories of great losses at the front. But they were optimistic, believing firmly in final victory.

Among them I met a young Pole with whom I walked for the hours, listening to the fascinating tale of the historic battle of Kutno in September 1939. The young man introduced himself, but unfortunately I have forgotten his name, which at the time I noted carefully in my diary. How well I remember his enthusiasm, hope and appetite for life, which enabled him to cross Asia in his attempt to reach the free world. I often wonder about his fate.

At last we received the necessary papers from the NKVD and with a friend from Oszmiana, Lola, my Latin teacher and her young son Andrzej, we bought tickets to Jangijul. This time it was a normal passenger train, although with no water and broken windows in several carriages. Railway travel was very complicated at that time in Russia. It was obligatory to get your ticket stamped at every change of train or junction. It was called "compasirowka biletow". In Pietropavlovsk we waited in long queues at the station, where we had to change to the "Trans Siberian" line to go westward to Ekaterinburg, formerly Sverdlovsk, and from there to Chelabinsk. We travelled west through the Ural mountains in bright sunshine and admired the beautiful scenery. At Ekaterinburg we changed trains again for the one going south to Tashkent in Uzbekistan, and again encountered the same complicated procedures. The landscape was now quite different. The steppes gave place to rich fields and orchards with fruit trees hanging with fruit. At the stations were huge mounds of water melons and cantaloupes for sale. We were able to buy them cheaply from the slowly moving train. The taste of the yellow melons was delicious.

In Tashkent we faced a real set back. Our train was diverted to a depot and although it was a short distance from Jangijul, we were stranded there. My mother's entreaties and patient persuasion were fruitless. Before boarding a train to resume our journey we had to produce not only the usual official stamp but also one from the disinfecting centre. I collected all our tickets and set off hopefully in search of that office. It was part of the public baths and quite a distance from the station. After enjoying a refreshing shower, I was given back my disinfected dress, or rather the remnants of it; the thin cotton was in shreds. At first they balked at stamping all the tickets, but finally did so and I began my return happily.

Walking in the gentle September sunshine I felt like a pilgrim, stopping in front of a huge mosque with its lofty minarets. The air was cooling and a yellow setting sun was reflected in the colourful mosaics. I experienced a sense of freedom and a desire to fly over that wonderful city.

Arriving at the station I was overtaken by panic. There was no sign of our train or my companions. Apparently, soon after I had left the ticket office, the train had been moved to another line. With the six tickets in my hand, but with no money, I felt lost and desperate. I run between the trains, searching for one going to Jangijul when I noticed two Polish soldiers about to board the Jangijul train. Hearing my cry of anguish they pulled me onto the carriage and hid me under a bench, until the controller left the compartment.

My tickets were not valid on this suburban train. Sitting between the two men in their woollen coats I felt warm and more optimistic. But the news they gave was very disturbing. Russia had withdrawn recognition of the Polish Refugee Centres and the army had to be evacuated. The alternative was incorporation into the Russian Army to fight the Germans from the East. Our army, they said, would leave Jangijul today and all civilians would be taken by force back to the kolkhozes.

The only departure camp was in Ashkabad, where they were going, and they advised me to go too. My heart sank. Approaching Jangijul, I saw in the dim light of station lamps and a sea of people spreading over the railway lines. The train was moving slowly through the mass of people and I watched, face glued to the window in the corridor. Suddenly, a shiver ran down my spine. I recognised a jumper, knitted by me in a clearly distinguishable style. It was my brother outside the window. Pushing passengers aside I jumped from the train and moments later I was with them. My mother was distressed and overtaken by grief. She was lying on the ground. Seeing me, she could not believe her eyes. "Thank God for this miracle", she said. Had I not recognised the jumper it would have been virtually impossible to find my family in those enormous crowds.

The Polish army was leaving Jangijul with banners and a band playing military tunes when mother and Lola arrived with children. Someone stole mother's case with my diary in it, but she found something to put over my poor dress. People around us were crying helplessly, terrified by the prospect of being forced to return to the place from which they had just escaped.

We camped on the lines for next few days and mother queued every day for hours at the police station, clutching papers and telegrams supposed to entitle her to be at the army centre. Somehow we were overlooked by the agents who were dragging people onto the lorries to take them back to the kolkhozes.

One day we heard a whisper that during the following night a transport of Polish orphans would be passing through Jangijul. This offered our last chance of escape if only we could get on it. It is difficult to recollect how it happened, but the train really did arrive. It moved slowly along our line and all of us, including Lola and her little boy, managed to get a foothold on the train. We pulled ourselves inside through windows with the help people inside. What a relief! The train was packed to the gunnels, but we were accepted and taken on board. I was put on a luggage shelf, mother and Lola found a seat, and the boys settled on the floor.

The journey to Ashkabad lasted four days. We had no food left and very little drinking water. Everybody stank from the heat and from the lack of washing and toilets. Approaching a bridge over a very big river, the train slowed to a crawl. I pushed to the front carriage and jumped off the train when it reached bridge, then rolled down the embankment, took a dip in the water and rushed back up the steep slope managing to jump onto the last carriage. It was madness, but I had to do it!

We reached Ashkabad one evening and were met by soldiers and an army canteen. Everybody was given a mug of black tea with the warning not to eat anything the next day, to drink black tea only for the twenty four hours. Then the lorries took us to the camp and we soon found ourselves in military tent with beds and blankets. What luxury!

The next morning we received our food rations and a tin opener. It was an impressive display of riches: canned beef, sardines, condensed milk, cheese, marmalade, drinking chocolate, canned fruit and more besides. I forgot the warnings of yesterday, and opened tins. To my mother's disapproval I tasted them all. How right she was! I certainly paid for it.

The following day we were back on the lorries and on our way to Persia – modern day Iran. The sensation of freedom was overwhelming and I felt it deeply, although I suffered from terrible indigestion. An important stage in "The School of Life" was over. I was ready and eager to meet the next stage.

III. TEHERAN 1942 – 1944

The long convoy of lorries with civilians from Ashkabad left Russia and crossed the border with cries of joy and relief. We traversed the Kopet Dag mountain chain in bright autumn sunshine travelling on a dangerously narrow, winding road. The skill of the drivers was entirely admirable; not even once did the convoy stop in order to put a vehicle back on to the road. The views were magnificent, with rocky ridges, deep gorges and splashing rapid torrents of water. It seemed that we entered PARADISE.

Towards the evening we arrived in the old town of Meshed where we were unloaded on the main square to make our first night stop. It was a big empty space, surrounded by small houses with beautiful gardens, full of flowering trees and exotic plants. Here, for the first time I saw pomegranats. In no time at all the square was covered with a layer of bodies, mine being on the outer edge. It was cold and the moon was rising over the roofs. For warmth we nestled closely together. I could not sleep and watched the moon, trying to imagine our future.

Suddenly, I saw a dark shadow drawing nearer to me. In my dreamy state it resembled the Hunchback of Notre Dame. When he bent over me I shut my eyes and held my breath in fear. Then I felt something weighty thrown over me. I opened my eyes and I saw "the shadow" repeating this ritual over other people. There were other "shadows" in the square, busy moving around until everyone was covered with a splendid Persian carpet. I sobbed with emotion, deeply touched by this gesture of comradeship.

In the rising sun the square looked bewitched. Like coloured waves the carpet–covered bodies began to move in ever changing patterns. We stacked the rugs in heaps at the corners of the square and boarded the lorries. The town of Meshed was still asleep.

The road to Teheran led through a rough, dry terrain. Each small village we passed seemed like an oasis. It was hot, the sun danced on the asphalt in fantastic images. Along the road people in long white tunics and turbans were waving to us, throwing bunches of fruit. On the way we were offered appetising food and drink, which made us even more eager to see the renowned city of Teheran.

Polish refugees were settled in three camps arranged on the outskirts of the town. Number one had a view of the white cap of snow at the top of Dermavent, the summit of the Elbrus mountains. The camp was surrounded by a wire fence and near the entrance stood a two storey red brick building, separated from the rows of barracks by a big open central area. We were allocated to a huge room on the first floor, furnished with lines of knee high wooden platforms and subdivided by hanging blankets into cubicles for individual families. Right away we were given articles of basic needs. Using two towels, I quickly made myself a simple dress and threw away my tattered, shredded one.

Life in the camp was very interesting and Teheran seemed absolutely fabulous. After settling down, the young ones enrolled at camp schools which taught accelerated courses in order to close the gap of lost years. People were moving around excitedly, looking for missing relatives and making new friendships. To our great joy we met aunt Janka from Kokchetav with cousins Krystyna and Busia. My father came from Iraq on a long leave and stayed in town, as did my uncle Bronislaw and Lola's husband. Most of the youth joined the scouts which gave them the opportunity to explore the town and the countryside. But I liked exploring on my own.

Teheran 1943. Reunited family!

One day I was approached by a middle aged woman whom I did not recognise at first. She was delighted and smiled nicely and embraced me with emotion, telling her companions about the hospitality we gave her family the previous year in Zoldubay. With moving words of gratitude she recalled the evening when they were stopped by me and my mother invited them to stay the night.

We had complete freedom of movement and no permission was required to pass through the gate. The journey to town was an enjoyable two kilometres, along a tree lined avenue which ended almost at the central square, with its beautiful fountain in front of parliament building and a nearby mosque covered with glittering, colourful tiles. There began the main street with its elegant shops, reaching to other parts of the city and the famous Persian Market. And what a wonder that was! The labyrinth of alleys with donkeys loaded with merchandise – and lots and lots of people. There were goods in metal, leather, silk, cotton and glass; there were precious stones, jewellery, carpets, lamps, mirrors and myriads of domestic items. There were stands displaying food of all kinds; vegetables and spices with strong, sometimes disturbing smells. In town some of the pavements were covered with new carpets and people were encouraged to walk on them, to "distress" them before sale. On my first visit I had the impression of an outlandish world of exotic colours, smells and faces. I was fascinated.

In the centre of Teheran, people looked prosperous. I saw beautiful women with eyes of gazelles and long, black, wavy hair falling over Persian lamb coats. They were wearing shoes with very high heels and knee length dresses exposing legs of various shapes and sizes. The men of the town looked almost European in their expensive suits, a good half being overweight, with rolling almond shaped eyes. I had some trouble with them when they passed along the street in their luxurious limousines, offering a lift. My hair had grown by now, so imagine a blond of seventeen in these surroundings. But I felt pretty safe, although I had to suffer the occasional pinch.

Beside the glamorous elite of Teheran there was a motley crowd of people – merchants, artisans, shopkeepers and drifters, some in white gowns and round caps. Some looked like warriors, with sharp faces, black beards, thin lips and dark eyes. I found them very intriguing and attractive, but most to my liking were the Armenians, who seemed to carry their tragic history visible in their demeanour. Although they are acknowledged to be masters of mathematics and engineering, most of them were employed as drivers in our camp. They became real friends and guardians, rescuing young girls from unpredicted crises during our perambulations. As a group of sympathetic visitors we discovered the poor districts, taking with us tins of conserves for the old women sitting in front of the dilapidated buildings. In return, they smiled, with a gesture for more.

Once walking alone between the camps I came on a very big property with magnificent trees visible above the surrounding walls. Walking round, I found the gate with an Armenian guard. I greeted him in a friendly manner and he invited me in, explaining that it was a hunting lodge of the Shah, who comes on Fridays before setting off for hunting in the mountains. On that day no one dare be there to interrupt the royal pleasure. The guard, probably bored with his solitude, offered me a conducted tour of the place. It was a dream like fairyland, full of exotic trees, flowers, fountains, cascades, rocks and statues, with an elegant round lodge on higher ground. It was a two storey building with a continuous balcony above harmonious colonnade, all in perfect proportion. We went to one corner of the garden which housed the Shah's small private zoo. The guard showed me the latest acquisition: two big tigers in a huge cage. He fed the animals and suggested that I might enter the lodge, provided I did not touch anything. Well, what a treat! I have never been surrounded by greater splendour and I felt like Cinderella herself. To my eyes everything was magic. The paintings on the walls and on the ceiling with rural motifs were beautiful. There were glittering mirrors in gilded frames, exquisite China vases, clocks, light, elegant furniture. I could not restrain myself from sitting on one of the chairs and, after wandering around for nearly an hour, I rejoined the guard at the gate, thanking him from the bottom of my heart. Then, with some hesitation, I asked if he would allow me to bring a few friends to see this "Fairy Land". He scratched his head, looked at me carefully and said "yes". But remember, it is a secret. And never on Friday! A week later seven trustworthy colleagues and I were allowed in. The second visit was as impressive as the first. My friends were enchanted.

Some time later, during a half–term break, fifteen girls from my class set off for a picnic in the nearest hills, about six kilometres from the camp. We clambered across rough ground and had to cross wide ditch, which we did by making a rope with our tied scarves. Arriving at the rocks, which looked like big termite mounds, we made a base camp. While the majority settled down to rest, five of the stronger ones, including me, started to scale the mountain. This was another "first time" for me. We came across rich flora and found some old bones among the rocks. We were nearing the top when we heard gun shots and noises coming from the camp. My hair stood on end: it was Friday!

Like the wind, we hurried down and found no–one there. There were traces of horses hoofs and some remnants of our refreshments. Because I was the class prefect, I was responsible. I ran to the camp. The setting sun was blinding yet I saw the small stones scattered around, rather colourless in the morning, were now full of pinks, yellows, purples, green and blues. They must have been semi–precious minerals. On reaching the camp I burst into the nearest barrack, where Lila lived, one of our group. I found her in bed, shivering. Tell me what happened, I asked. "Well after you went off we were preparing the picnic, talking and joking, singing and dancing, when suddenly we were surrounded by a group of horsemen accompanied by two ladies. They were very smartly dressed, and so were the horses. Their guns frightened us and we hid in a panic behind the rocks. This probably amused the hunters who began to chase us around the rocks and some girls were picked up onto the saddles. After a while it stopped and we were told to return immediately to the camp. They explained in perfect English that it was the Shah's hunting party, although he was not with them that day. I think that one woman was his wife and her lady–in–waiting and a brother of the Shah with his friends". Poor Lila was shaken by this encounter with Persian royalty. I was relieved that no harm came to the girls and nothing was mentioned on return to school on Monday.

On another occasion our class went on a study excursion with the professor whom I adored because of his voice and his amiable personality. We were observing various living creatures in the stream which watered the fields before stopping at a big reservoir. A number of men were sitting at the edge with their feet dangling over the water. At one moment a sandal slipped from the foot of a villager and the professor, seeing it, called: "jump in and recover it!" I do not like diving, but I could not refuse, so I went head down to the bottom of the reservoir which was full of weed, mud and rubbish and worked through it till I found the sandal, then surfaced triumphantly. Climbing over the edge I sensed a sharp sting on my right palm. The professor looked at it: "Scorpion", he said and hurried us back to the camp, glancing from time to time at my hand. The bluish black line was moving to my wrist, slowly rising to my elbow. We ran back to the camp's hospital just in time for treatment. I was told, "bit later and amputation would be necessary".

I liked our school very much. The teachers, whom we called professors, were of a high standard and full of enthusiasm, which infected us all. Lola was teaching Latin, and the professor whom I liked so much, was an excellent teacher of Polish language. We knew him before the war in Lida, where he was a deputy to the Sejm (parliament) and a speaker of great renown. I did not know the others but they had a way of captivating the students with their subjects. My weakest subject was mathematics and I had to concentrate very hard in order to pass the grades.

We had less in common with the teacher of religion, who was an army chaplain. We found him rather soft and naive and we played a naughty trick on him. We removed the list of names from the class register and replaced it with a list of fictitious ones, all taken from the garden, ie. Miss Carrot, Potato, Beetroot, Cabbage, Onion etc. The Christian names were also changed to old fashioned ones like Hermenegilda, Honorata, Anastasia and so on.

We managed to convince him that we came from the same village and we were the daughters of the village baker, smith, butcher, postman. Everybody could see it was a joke, but not our priest. It continued through the whole term until the teachers' conference, where our priest read the notes against our names. I wish I could have seen his face!

The consequences were more than unpleasant. Our parents were called in and the class was suspended for a week. We never saw that priest at school again. I remember what my parents used to say. In their time it was the custom to send the brightest children to universities, the less bright to the army and the least bright into the church.

Scouting was well organised and my brothers, cousins and I were ardent members. We spent much time in Shemran, a big recreation centre outside Teheran, near the mountains, among enormous trees and rapid torrents. We swam in spacious pools, played games and organised excursions. There were also exciting night events with torches, searching for hidden treasure and other games. The scouts' and girl guides' Jamboree in Jussuf Abad was a special event. The main organizers were young officers delegated by the army. There were memorable evenings around campfires, singing, improvising spectacles or listening to fantastic tales. One of most attractive organisers was Rys, an energetic, handsome scout who had a magnificent voice, and the older Zygmunt, who introduced us to the southern sky and the magnitudes of stars. Others ran daily games and exercises, all geared to the building of our personalities in line with the slogan "healthy in spirit, healthy in body".

Of course there were also small intrigues and arguments. One remains in my memory. It happened during the Shah's twenty sixth birthday celebrations at the Teheran sports stadium. A small group of Polish girl guides was invited to form a guard of honour at the entrance. We went there with a large bouquet of flowers for the queen, and Wanda, a lovely girl with long plaits was chosen to present them. As she was descending from the jeep, a smart Danuta offered Wanda to hold the flowers while she was stepping down, but she would not return them. Ignoring our protests, she held on to them tight and, on the arrival of the royal couple, presented them to the queen with a nice courtesy. I noticed that queen Fawzia was not wearing any jewellery except for her wedding ring, which to me was a sign of great tact.

For us Poles, a most memorable day was the visit of General Sikorski who came from London to inspect the Polish forces stationed in the Middle East. Our camp served as a parade ground where all the military units and many civilians from other camps were assembled. The general walked past the ranks of soldiers, scouts and other organizations with his daughter at his side. It was only a few days before the fatal accident at Gibraltar on the 4 July 1943 in which both of them were killed.

By the end of the year the refugee camps were diminishing and civilians were distributed to other centres in different parts of the world. Mexico interested me very much so I put it on the top of my list of preferences, with Africa in second place. Most of my school friends were destined for India, the orphans to New Zealand, while quite a big group of the girls who had completed secondary school, went to study at the American University of Beirut. Among them was Ada, whom I admired very much.

My father left for Iraq and I had to promise to take care of my mother and my brothers, as well as continue my education. In the event we had no choice. We were destined for Uganda in Africa where my uncle Bronislaw was posted to run a hospital in one of the refugee settlements. Before departure, Lola managed to organize a school trip to Persepolis, one of the capitals of ancient Persia, founded in the sixth century B.C. The vast ruins were a truly memorable sight.

We left Teheran, my paradise, in the spring of 1944 for a transit camp near Ahwaz, by the wide river Kozun. The camp was situated at the top of sand dunes, so we were always covered in sand and our teeth would be grinding the stuff when we ate our meals in the camp canteen. Worst of all were the sand storms. I remember vividly how we had to cover our heads and even so the sand got into our ears, noses and eyes. Our few days stop stretched into weeks. I fell ill with dysentery and was taken to hospital.

Medical care there was poor and I was getting weaker every day, until the visit of my close school friend Zosia who brought a cure prepared by her mother. The sachets of powdered tea had miraculous effect and two days later I could once again stand on my feet. I left hospital secretly, staggering along the sandy bank of the river up to the camp. I spent that night on a camp bed outside the barracks, under the shining stars. The following day we climbed on to lorries and were driven to the port. I was lucky to be back in time, thanks to Zosia, she remained in Ahwaz with her mother and two sisters, awaiting transport to India.

At the port soldiers in English uniforms served us breakfast from the navy canteen on the pier. When my turn came I was handed a mug of tea and a bowl of porridge. Pointing at the porridge the soldier asked: "sugar"? "No, salt please" I said, at which he asked "Are you Scottish?" I shook my head and wondered about his question, unfamiliar with the Scottish custom. The tea was very thick, more like soup with milk, but I have been drinking "white tea" as long as I could remember.

The boat awaiting us was an old cargo ship, very uninviting and altogether unsuitable for a human cargo of two thousand. In the middle of the Persian Gulf anchor was lowered and the ship was immobilized for a week on the account of mines in the Indian Ocean. Our bodies were covered with itching rashes, aggravated by showers of salt water, as fresh water was reserved strictly for drinking. People were moving across the decks like robots, perspiration dripping from their bodies. Two old women died and were buried at sea. It was depressing.

From that miserable week I retained a wonderful story told by one of the passengers. Pointing west to the visible shores of Saudi Arabia he described vividly a marvellous oasis in the rocky Sinai desert with the beautiful old monastery of St. Catherine with its priceless treasures. "You can see there the oldest manuscripts of our civilisation and the most fabulous icons ever painted". He described the monastery with feeling and in such striking detail that it has remained in my mind. I promised myself I would visit the place one day. Half a century later I did visit that wondrous city, built by Justinian in the sixth century, and experienced the feeling of having been there before.

When at last anchor was raised and the boat moved the air freshened and our depressive mood changed. We watched dolphins playing in the water and the endless seascape of waves meeting the sky at the horizon. It was a long voyage with one stop at Bombay where a small group of refugees stepped off the boat to the waiting lorries. We could see the houses, the domed roofs of Indian temples and the beautiful palm trees. I wanted to go there, just for a minute, but it was out of the question. It produced the first sad feeling that my new freedom had limitations. Crossing the ocean for another week in the terrible heat and burning sun took its toll, until we finally reached Mombasa.

On the way, in mid–ocean, we were struck by a frightful storm. Huge waves lifted the boat almost clear of he water, dropped it with an enormous crash back on the sea. Most people were lying flat on the deck. Very few, like my mother and myself, carried on as usual, without missing a meal. The sea journey seemed never ending and monotonous. Our eyes searched for some sign of life in this infinity of water and horizon. The nights offered a magnificent display of the constellations and we enjoyed learning the names of individual stars. During the day any movement in the water or in the air was keenly observed and produced animated comments. These last days on the Indian Ocean passed with increasing impatience and growing expectations of Africa.

IV. UGANDA 1944 – 1948

With great expectations we were approaching the Black Continent. To my surprise Mombasa had a very European look from the distance, with its tall buildings and red tiled roofs. What a disappointment, I thought. But not for long. A few hours later our train passed through the most magnificent, dense jungle. Slowly the train climbed up to a cooler plateau, running across open savannah. Here people looked less dark, more coffee colour. Men of a warrior type were wrapped in bright red blankets, women wore high collars of colourful beads. They were the Massai. On the horizon to the left appeared a high mountain with a white snowy cap – it was Kilimanjaro. The train stopped at the foot of the mountain and the group of the orphans travelling with us stepped down into the arms of nuns waiting for them at the station. They were the Sisters of Nazareth, dressed in long black frocks and huge white bonnets.

About half way between Mombasa and Nairobi the train stopped at Makindu station and we were told to get off with our hand luggage. We were led to a fenced camp recently vacated by Italian prisoners of war. It consisted of almost hundred light huts with a big open space in the middle and a complex of brick buildings along one side. We were to rest there for a week, reason unknown. Inside the huts were wooden benches and mattresses, but nothing else. Our luggage was kept locked on the train for the night and we prepared ourselves for our first night in Africa. Trusting the tropical climate we were looking for a good night's sleep without covers. In the morning I woke up finding myself underneath the mattress on the bare slats. The night had turned cold and unconsciously I must have scrambled under the mattress.

The luggage was brought by a number of ebony coloured boys and we settled in for our temporary stay at camp. The commandant was an oldish English colonel, who assured us that the barbed wire fence was for our protection. He was obsessed with hunting wild animals and when we heard that he needed helpers to carry ammunition boxes, I with two other scouts volunteered. But he did not tolerate women on his outings so some imagination was brought to play. I disguised myself as a boy- not difficult with my short hair and scout uniform. I could not loose such an opportunity! We set off to the savannah in a jeep and my heart was beating fast with excitement. My eyes wide open in anticipation and with difficulty I controlled my girlish outbursts of delight.

Till now Africa was a fiction of my imagination, stimulated by books and films. Now it was real, with me right there! Zigzagging between huge trees and through dense undergrowth we gradually emerged into open space where we began to encounter the animals. It was like a magnificent show. Among the occasional acacia and some shrubs a herd of zebra was grazing, suddenly turning at the sound of our motor and showing us their striped rears. Monkeys were busy swinging from branch to branch, leaping from one tree to another right above our heads to the other side of the track. Some giraffes, beautiful and majestic, broke into a run and passed us like a well rehearsed ballet troupe with harmonious body movement, their delicate heads swaying on long necks. There were groups of graceful gazelles, ever alert for impending danger. On the dead branches of a rugged tree vultures were sitting, surveying the scene.

Suddenly the colonel stopped the car, pointing to the big herd of buffalo in the distance. He stepped down, giving us the sign to follow with the boxes and to be quiet with it. He ran with such speed towards the buffalo that it was difficult to keep up with him. Then we witnessed a phenomenal sight: few hundred meters away the huge animals formed a perfect quadrangle with about thirty males on the outside and cows were grouped inside. They watched our colonel rushing through savannah until, as at one command, the entire herd made a ninety degree turn and galloped in the direction of the nearby forest, with the colonel trying to keep up with them. In a few minutes they were out of sight.

It was a strange feeling of being deserted. We waited alone and were suddenly stricken with fear by the appearance of an approaching rhinoceros. It was ambling along without hurry, resembling a blown up sausage on short legs with a projecting muzzle – its precious horn. The boys were muttering panicky suggestions to run, but there was nowhere to go, there were no trees near us. We were not sure if the rhino could smell us. But we knew the rhino has very poor eye sight so we stayed behind the bush and kept our fingers crossed. We were lucky. The massive animal continued his even paced trot and passed us few meters away. We breathed a sign of relief.

The colonel emerged from the woods in a very bad temper, empty handed. Later he was taking aim at a gazelle, then at a zebra without any success. Without any meat for the camp kitchen the return drive was made in a sombre mood. He had never experienced such bad luck as today except on one occasion, when a woman friend was in the party. I kept quiet. Feeling slightly guilty, I never again sought the job of ammunition carrier.

The camp cooks were feeding us generously, even with no meat on the menu. Their stews of pumpkin, maniok, aubergines and various beans were very tasty and the African fruits were delicious. A novelty for us were local mangoes, small, round and very sweet, and the papayas and passion fruit. Peanuts were plentiful and we roasted them ourselves. A number of peanuts plantations were in the vicinity.

The hunting expedition gave me a taste for wild life outside the camp and aroused an appetite for further explorations. Not far from Makindu was a Nature Reserve with an observation platform over a watering place, a centre of nocturnal life. I obtained permission to take a group of girl–guides on a two day excursion. The condition was that a grown–up person should accompany us, and my aunt Janka eagerly agreed. After the essential preparations and the wait for a full moon, we left camp loaded with provisions, torches, ropes, blankets and a detailed map as well as a code of behaviour, featuring a long list of don'ts.

A path of about ten miles led through the savannah, then through giant grass known as elephant grass, and finally through dense jungle with the enormous trees and thick lianas. A few boy scouts joined us along the way and we arrived at the tree platform in early afternoon. There was a large clearance around a wonderful baobab tree with a watering place next to it, all surrounded by a wall of elephant grass. From the tree a rope ladder was hanging, at the top of it was a wooden platform with a balustrade encircling the colossal trunk, about ten feet above ground. The scene was deserted, the water hole as big as a large swimming pool was still, with no sign of life. We made a short exploratory walk around then cooked our meal over the fire and finished the day with the usual singing around log fire. Before sunset we extinguished the fire, climbed the ladder and pulled it up. The platform was not big enough for everyone, it was designed for a maximum of twelve persons and there were sixteen of us. The boys decided to tie themselves with ropes to the strong branches. Nobody was able to sleep that night. Full of excitement, we waited for the moon and listened to the noises.

It was not yet completely dark, although close to the equator night falls almost simultaneously with the setting sun. Then we heard a roar near our tree. Two lions were circling it furiously with their huge heads turned up towards us. They tried to climb the tree, scratching at the trunk, but the tree defeated them and eventually they went away. While the moon was rising we lined up along the balustrade. The jungle was awakening with the sounds of birds and animals. Into our view came long chain of elephants joined together by their trunks holding the tail of ones in front. They moved majestically towards the water place. The sight was breathtaking. Some of them were enormous, bur there were also several endearing baby elephants. After spending about half an hour drinking and spraying themselves with water, they made room for other animals. This seemed to be an established order because without any congestion one species followed another without any aggravation or struggle. After zebras came gazelles, then giraffes, and at about midnight the rhinos. They were not in a friendly mood, but were fighting furiously in the middle of the hole, half submerged. This was quite a spectacle; with anger and jealousy (or was it fun?) they were attacking each other emitting loud nasal noises, their horns poking into an opponent's thick skin. They created a turbulence in the pool that lasted for quite a while until they left, exhausted, each in different direction. Later in the night some more elephants appeared on the scene. It was a piece of rare theatre for us, watching safely from our platform.

At sunrise we dropped the rope ladder and climbed down for a wash in the water we brought from the camp. While breakfast was being prepared I jumped into the pool even though the water was muddy and overgrown with plants. It was refreshing and invigorating. My aunt cried out, horrified: "What are you doing? There may be snakes!" I don't see any, I answered calmly and promptly got out. Well, it was thoughtless, I had to admit, I had no fears about the depth of the pool – the short legs of rhino had revealed that last night.

After breakfast we prepared games for the day. The girls split into two teams and went to collect samples of tree bark, grass, bones and animal droppings. In two hours they were to meet me at an agreed spot in a clearing not far from our base. My aunt stayed behind to rest after her sleepless night. The boys did their own exploration.

Before leaving the camp the commandant assured me, that during the day the animals went quite far away from the water hole and it would be safe. Waiting at the meeting point by a broken tree in the middle of clearing, I was contemplating recent events when I heard a noise through the long grass. Suddenly it opened to reveal two Africans running. They were spectacular! Faces painted in white patterns, their shining black bodies draped with an animal skin and feather helmets on their heads, in one hand an oval shaped painted shield, a long spear in the other. Around their ankles were colourful beads. They were running rhythmically over the clearing and I watched them bewildered, but entirely unafraid. I am sure they saw me, but they passed without giving any sign and disappeared in the high wall of elephant grass.

Their behaviour was immensely impressive. Was it an expression of natural freedom or an admirable tolerance of strangers? They were beautiful and seemed to enjoy my admiring gaze. Never before or since have I seen anything to equal the spectacle. I wondered about my girls. Had they met these two Africans, were they frightened? They arrived half an hour later from their reconnaissance trip. Happy with their findings, but not mentioning anything unusual. We returned to our base singing to enjoy lunch, a siesta, and another camp fire.

The second night was similar to the first one. The lions came angrily circling the tree again, then after a drink at the water hole, disappeared. Again in turns came the elephants, zebras, and gazelles, followed by giraffes and the rhinos at midnight. This time their visit was beautiful. We slept soundly and after breakfast we packed up and marched back to the camp. The girls were talking in low voices, exchanging impressions and observations, halting sometimes to better recall a detail. My aunt had no complaints and the commandant was glad to see us safe and sound.

The next day we all received information about the last leg of the journey. All our luggage was to be gathered on the main square than taken to the train by local boys. Returning from a last walk outside the camp I saw above the hut a black cloud with red flames shooting in the sky. Frightened, I ran back to our barrack fending off pieces of burning tarred paper, which was flying in all directions. My mother was trying desperately to drag our chest from the burning hut. Together we managed to do it just in time, dumping it safely in the square.

In one hour the roofs and the walls had burned down and the camp looked like forest of smouldering wooden posts. The smell of burnt tar was very oppressive and black soot was covering everything. Luckily there were no victims and we spent our last night in Makindu under the stars.

With great relief we boarded the train the next morning. The railway line ran along the Reserve and I watched with astonishment the long–legged ostriches racing the train. At Nairobi station we had a few hours stop, and I took the chance for a short walk to town to see the capital of Kenya. Not enough time to reach the centre, my main recollection now is an enormous turtle in the garden of a colonial residence.

We continued through Jinja on the equator to Kampala, capital of Uganda. Lorries took us from there to our final destination, the settlement of Koja on a peninsula on Lake Victoria. The little white houses encircling a small church at the top of the plateau looked very picturesque.

The settlement was built only a few years before our arrival and we were the latest addition to a population of about two thousand. My family was allocated a house with a pretty porch in the lowest lane close to the lagoon. The house consisted of three rooms, one of which had a separate entrance and was occupied by a very special lady, a beautician from Lvov. She was preoccupied with concerns about the condition of her body, especially her complexion.

The interior was modestly furnished with beds and bedding, a table and a few chairs. Outside was a little hut for cooking and a toilet. We were instructed to put the legs of the beds in tins of paraffin to stop insects from crawling up the legs of the beds. Of course we also had a mosquito net. Uncle Bronislaw with his family was housed in an attractive villa near the hospital.

The first few days were blissful. The air, the space, the lagoon and the powerful green jungle behind was like the setting of an exotic film.

My mother and brothers by the lagoon

We were given our food rations and a little pocket money which enabled us to begin an independent existence. But within a few days most of us experienced a strange itching at the tips of our fingers and toes, which increased daily and kept us awake at night. This was caused by tiny insects laying their eggs under our nails and nothing could be done until their incubation two weeks later. It was the customary initiating treat for newcomers to Koja.

The settlement had a small secondary school, but for the last two years we had to move to the Lyceum at Masindi. It was a modest boarding school, modelled on the English system. It was in a complex of several buildings just outside the village settlement, consisting of about a dozen of long structures. The dormitories accommodated up to twenty girls and a guardian. The central building which looked like a huge barn was our dining hall.

The dormitory was subdivided by blanket screens into two person cubicles and I shared one with my cousin, Krystina, who became my great friend. The food at the boarding school was really very poor. First we had bean soup followed by beans as the main course, often with white maggots enriching it. Dessert was a bean compote. No doubt we occasionally had better dishes, but memory of their taste faded away over the years. The houses were set in pleasant, park–like grounds, with lawns and a number of charming papaya trees with fruits the size and shape of rugby balls hanging around their slender trunks below an umbrella of long leaves. Two years spent in Masindi were dull. There was very little excitement.

One morning, I woke up feeling of being airborne. Indeed, my bed was about half a meter above the floor, balancing on top of a termite mound. The termites went through all my books which were under the bed and devoured the paper, leaving only the strips with the metal clips. Another diversion was provided by the snake, quite a long one but fortunately not poisonous.

One incident broke the placid atmosphere. When the village officials decided to remove all stray dogs from the school compound, we were worried about our shaggy, three legged Morus, a favourite of everyone. I saw two men dragging him towards the forest behind our dormitory. With Krystina I followed them through the shrubs and when the men returned, we ran into the woods. Not far from the edge we saw our Morus hanging from a thick branch of a baobab. Stretching up I managed to lift his bottom up with my finger tips until Krystina returned with a knife and a stool. We cut the rope and carried his motionless body back to our dormitory, checked his heart and found it was beating, then poured a little water through his clenched teeth and put him tenderly underneath my bed. In the night, I was awakened by a scratching noise and saw him trying to climb through the mosquito netting. Before leaving for school I shared my secret with the guardian, fed him and tied him to the leg of my bed with the joined up belts of our dressing gowns.

The school was a row of structures each side of a wide path with the classes in each building. The walls came half way up, with timber posts rising at even intervals to support the roof. Later that day the sound of loud laughter was heard from the class at the other end of the complex. There was our Morus, walking slowly along the path dragging a long colourful tail of gorgeous dressing gown belts behind him. He came straight to my class and sat under my desk. The news of the miraculous recovery of a hanged dog spread quickly through the school and I was called to the office. I was given a paper which stated that I was the official owner of Morus and that he was no stray dog. So we lived happily together till my graduation.

A year later I visited Masindi, where my brother Janusz was taking his final year. The bus from Kampala arrived rather late in the evening and a moment after descending something heavy pushed me to the ground. It was Morus, full of excitement. He was then in the care of a younger colleague. This was the last time I saw him and I often wondered what happened to him when the settlement closed down.

One of the pleasant events in Masindi was the wedding of a girl in my class, Danuta. She was exceptionally good – looking, with a divinely beautiful face. She married our teacher of Polish, an ascetic figure resembling a poet – philosopher. At least that's how I saw him. They caused me to dream of my own future.

After graduation I took the bus to Kampala before joining my mother in Koja. The first part of this journey is worth recording. The buses in Uganda had the first row of seats behind the driver reserved for non–Africans, with an expanded metal screen separating them from others. I was alone on the front bench until the arrival of a middle aged Indian and his big bunch of bananas and bundle wrapped in a blanket. We sat in silence while the rear of the bus resembled a bee hive. Suddenly, in the middle of the jungle, the bus stopped with smoke and flames belching from the engine. Panic–stricken Africans abandoned the bus, the driver helped me out with my case. The passengers and their belongings scattered along the road as I sat beside a woman with several children. The repairs took many hours so we reached Kampala about midnight.

The bus station was closed and deserted except for some beggars and some unfortunates. I had instructions to go to the house of Polish refugees, but had no address, and there was nobody available to make enquiries. I looked around, then I saw my Indian companion waving at me and at the young African who was to take my case. He beckoned me to follow him. We criss –crossed the town, the Indian stopping frequently to knock on gates, talking and taking something out of his bundle. I began to feel suspicious and scary thoughts crossed my mind. Finally, he stopped in front of an attractive villa, pointing with a polite gesture to the plate bearing the name: Polish House. He knocked on the door, waited for it to open, the boy put down my case and then they both disappeared into the darkness before I had a chance to thank them. A sleepy woman came out, embraced me affectionately and led me inside. She gave me a glass of beer and slowly my apprehension turned to joy and my tension was released.

The next day I went to Koja to stay with my mother for a week before going to Tengeru, the biggest Polish refugee settlement in Africa where the authorities organised a teaching course. It was a very poor substitute for my dream of studying in Johannesburg, but it was another step towards independence. Tengeru was situated at the foot of Mount Kenya. I liked my new surroundings and enjoyed meeting up again with a number of my friends from Teheran. The two months course was very intensive. We had very few outings, but they included one to an old monastery on the slopes of Mount Kenya. Another one took us to a beautiful crater lake; the whole area had a volcanic history. There were pleasure boats for crossing the lake but I preferred to swim across. When I came out of the water I heard my friends frantic shouting. "What is the matter?" I asked. "If only you could see your back, it is black with leeches!" Some were dropping off, sated with my blood others had to be taken off by my friends, but I felt nothing.

After the course finished we returned to Kampala on the train. During the journey the girls were in a festive mood, but I was glum. It was my twentieth birthday. I had the overwhelming feeling that my youth was over and that I was not yet ready for adulthood. Upon arrival in Koja we received important infor-

Lady Tarzan?

mation regarding our work placement. I was designated to teach three subjects in a secondary school: Latin, mathematics and Polish. It was a great shock to me. For what sins am I punished, I asked myself. Did I have to pay for my love of Ovid, Cicero and Seneca, or my declamation in hexameters when participating in school events? Mathematics has always been my Achilles heel! Why was such a load thrown on my shoulders?

Sleepless nights accompanied my preparation of the lessons. When the class started children were addressing me "Pani Professor" (Madame Professor). I explained that I had no right to this title as I did not have a university degree. Their reaction was disarming: "But we want to have a professor!" So I gave in.

Then it went from bad to worse. The seniors of the settlement asked me to join the local Council. "We need a young mind", said my uncle. The atmosphere was very provincial and obviously they were trying to inject some life into it. Among other duties I had to read bulletins of world news in the village hall. It all seemed very humdrum and routine, so I began to look for new distractions.

I fell in love with Lake Victoria. This was where I spent most of my free time. Swimming in the lake was officially forbidden because of the danger of Bilharzia and crocodiles. I always stressed this danger to my pupils, but I myself did not heed the warning. While swimming I hid my clothes and only my closest friends knew of my insubordinate daring.

Of course, there were some unexpected moments. After one afternoon's swim I climbed up small rock which projected from the shore. Then I spotted its serrated shape and rough texture and realised it was a crocodile's tail. Panic stricken I slid silently back into the water, clenching my fists in preparation for a struggle. I had heard that the most effective tactic was a strong punch into its soft belly. But the crocodile was motionless, it was fast asleep – as it was its siesta time. Someone had told me that this was the safest time to be in the water.

On another occasion, returning from a swim, I found two village guards waiting for me over my hidden clothes. They bombarded me with questions: "Your name? How old are you? Where you live? What school you go to?" Luckily they took me for a school girl. "You will have to kill me first before you will have these details" I said, then quickly picked up my things and ran. Poor dears, they were quite old and soon gave up the chase. For the next few days I resisted the temptation to swim.

One Sunday morning a terrible accident happened in our lagoon. From the porch I watched three boys swimming away from the shore. Suddenly two of them swam back. The third, who was ahead of the others looked around and not seeing his companions, decided to turn too. Then I saw him flung into the air by a blow from a crocodile's tail and then fall straight into the reptile open jaws. It dragged the boy to the opposite side of the lagoon, submerging and resurfacing at intervals. Then I saw a fountain of sand shoot up where the crocodile was putting his prey into storage; that was the burial place of the poor twelve year old orphan Sliva.

The boys who escaped sounded the alarm and people came to the lake, lamenting. We were looking for the scouts boat, but "Panna Wodna" (our sailing boat) was on the other side of the village, so we paddled in an old wreck to the scene of accident. We searched and dived, but could not find any trace of the boy. The whole village was mourning.

A few days later we were awoken in early morning by a great uproar at the end of our lagoon and we saw a crocodile making violent jumps out of the water. A strong rope was attached to a big tree near the shore and the other end of it came out of the jaws of the beast. It turned out that Mr. Kulka, the village shoemaker, determined to revenge young Sliva, has set up a dead cat with a hook as a bait. We helped him to pull the reptile, now dead, onto the grass. There he stood, with a bottle of vodka surveying his two meters long victim. He allowed himself to be photographed with the beast and with the ladies of Koja. I have a photo of my mother sitting on the creature.

Victoria on the crocodile

Krystina and Janusz returned from Masindi after their graduation and Janusz worked at the secretariat of the grammar school, where he also taught. My younger brother Tadzik was a pupil in my class, struggling with Latin. All of us, including our cousins Busia and Krystina, were active in scouting. I was second in command of the girl guides, while Janusz was in charge of boys under the supervision of Ignac, an instructor delegated from headquarters in London. The chief of the girls was Lunia.

During school holidays we enjoyed camping trips, on foot or on our sailing boat "Panna Wodna" to small island on the lake. We searched for flamingos and tortoises. Once we found such an enormous baobab tree that fifteen girls could not embrace its trunk. On another occasion a group of older girls and a troop–leader set off for a few days walking safari to Kampala and Entebbe.

We were travelling partly through wilderness and partly along the roads and where we were very tired, accepted a lift from a passing lorry. We had to lie flat not to be seen as it was forbidden to have any contact with the natives. We stopped at the catholic mission in Namiliango where during the school break, dormitories were empty. We used them to rest and tend our blistered feet. The mission was set in a magnificent landscape, with big lawns between the brick buildings of the school, the chapel, the dining hall and the library. Adjoining were some farm outbuildings with a kitchen garden behind. One sight is still vivid in my memory. Two little African girls were crossing the lawn when they met two white nuns. The girls went down on their knees and kissed the outstretched hands of the nuns, remaining on their knees until the nuns had disappeared in the distance. Thoughts of slavery passed through my mind. Was it right to keep the Africans in such a submissive state?

Actually we had very little contacts with the native population. My brothers visited the nearest village but I never went with them. Often in the evenings we heard "tam–tams" and some terrifying stories, but in general we had an agreeable relationship with the African authorities. Kabaka, the ruler of Uganda, let us have our scouting camp on his territory. He came to pay us a visit and gazed with great fascination at the golden hair of Olenka, whom he called Oruk.

On the subject of camps, one day the three of us, Lunia, Ignac and myself sailed in "Panna Wodna" in search of suitable camping site. The weather was fine and with gentle wind we sailed smoothly across the lake. Unfortunately on the way back the wind dropped completely. The boat scarcely moved and we used the little paddles we found on the bottom of the boat. We were miles from Koja where we saw the lights coming on in the houses and then being extinguished for the night. Eventually, at four in the morning, we dropped the anchor in Koja. Lunia's mother was waiting on the pier trembling with anxiety after pacing the shore most of the night. I hurried across the village to our house and was relieved to find Mama soundly asleep in bed. She awakened on my noisy entrance. "Were you worried?" I asked. With a smile she answered "No, I have a great confidence in your good sense and anyway, worrying would not solve anything". She had a wonderfully philosophical mind, our mother.

"Panna Wodna"

On another occasion I went with my young cousin Busia and Tadzik in a small boat across the lagoon to collect some papyruses when suddenly a young hippo emerged from the thicket and swam towards us. We turned the boat but the hippo kept swimming parallel with us. Fear seized us knowing about the peculiar solidarity between hippopotamus and crocodile. The first overturns the boat and the second attacks. Luckily our hippo soon tired of us, returning towards the thicket.

Often hippos came at night to the village cabbage field, situated between the lowest lane and the lagoon. Cultivation there had to stop because the cabbage was eaten and the site became full of round holes, more than half a meter deep, punched by the hippos feet. We saw them from our porch and heard their snorting and joked about their similarity to big cows.

The most popular local vegetable was manioc root, which replaced the potato, grated, mixed with egg and fried, it tasted very much like potato pancakes. Fried bananas were also very much appreciated as were the compotes of various fruits. Besides the small sweet banana with a slight strawberry taste, there were oranges, rather small and greenish and not very juicy, marvellous papayas (delicious with lemon and sugar); guavas, pineapples, and the Rolls Royce of all fruits – the mango. Not as we know it from today's supermarkets, but smallish, yellow, fibrous and sweet with a tinge of pine resin.

We quickly adopted the local way of eating pineapples, and walked with slices of this wonderful fruit cut in half and held in both hands. Local markets were very attractive places, the people often being more interesting than the merchandise. Women from Uganda were reminiscent of Greek Caryatides, with their baskets of goods resting upon their heads. Wrapped in colourful cotton shifts from the bust down, their beautiful shoulders supported strong necks and well shaped heads with sensual features.

I did not find men so interesting. Quite a number worked in the settlement as sweepers of the sandy lanes, drivers of village carts, or as domestic servants. My aunt had to keep the food cupboard locked, because her "boy" was very keen on tasting its contents. She trained him well and for his good efforts he would receive a big basket of provisions for his family. At least once a week local fisherman brought in fresh water fish of great variety of shape and size.

There were no newspapers, no radio or telephone in the village so life went on with little knowledge of the rest of the world. The religious customs were observed with great devotion. The absence of men was our misfortune and I was sorry for our mothers, still young and lonely. There were rumours of an occasional liaison with older school boys. Even the priests had to guard themselves from the attention of worshipping females.

The young people participated in all activities of the settlement, sometimes improvising theatrical events. The culmination of this was a performance of the classic play by the eighteenth century writer Fredro, the comedy "Sluby Panienskie" (Maidens' Vows) parodying the backwardness of the Sarmatian nobility. After several rehearsals all went smoothly. The actors were highly excited and the gifted artist, Czeslawa, prepared a beautiful stage set. The cast included a seventeen year old Janusz, who played the main role of Gustaw the seducer, not too convincingly though. I had no experience in matters of courtship so I asked Ignac to coach him. The performance was very successful and for few days the comedy was played to full houses in our village hall. The actors were reluctant to leave the stage – they enjoyed wearing the skilfully made period costumes.

As a result of my frequent contact with the water in the lake I landed in hospital with bilharzias, a parasitic flat worm, which consumes red blood cells. The only effective treatment was a blood transfusion, not possible in our hospital, only available in Nairobi where it was not accessible to refugees. My uncle decided to keep me in the village hospital under his constant supervision. I do not know what treatment he provided, but over a month later when the proportion of red to white cells improved, he discharged me, saying that my strong constitution would do what was needed to bring my blood to the required equilibrium. Before bilharzias I had a strong attack of malaria suffered by most of the community. The lake was a breeding ground for mosquitoes and it was beyond us to eliminate them. Their effect was painful and irritating. The cold sweats were particularly distressing.

The school organised an all day excursion to Kampala. We visited the museum, the cathedral and the university. The art department had very impressive exhibits of stone and wood carvings. Most of the girls ran to the shops to buy their first lipsticks and to look in the shop windows. I bought a big watch "Cyma" more suitable for a man, but I wanted one which I could easily see in the dark.

I kept in touch by mail with some of my friends from Masindi and heard their stories of romance. I also had my hero, Richard, who was sending me almost daily reports from Monte Casino. We lived in the same house in Grodno before the war, and his father, when with the army in the Middle East, sent me parcels of nice fabrics. He was treating me as his future daughter–in law. So I thrived on my imagination until the day a letter arrived from Richard with a photo of a beautiful girl – his fiancé. The earth shook under my feet and the sun darkened. But after the war, during my first visit to Poland, I met him unexpectedly – and thanked my fate! He was not the man of my dreams at all.

Early in 1948 came a rumour that the refugee camps were to close and my mother was called to the office. She had to prepare to join her husband in England with her sons. But I was excluded because I was already over twenty one and therefore an adult. We had been in constant correspondence with my father and knew that he was stationed in Scotland at the end of the war. Later he was to finish his course at a Polish faculty of law in Oxford. I wanted very much to return to Poland but the Poland I knew, of Wilno, Grodno, Lida and Oszmiana, was now part of the USSR. I had no home. What an irony, I thought. England, who played a role in giving Poland to Stalin was now accepting Polish ex–servicemen and thousands of civilians. Was it in recognition of the bravery of our pilots, sailors and soldiers who fought on the side of the Allies?

I accompanied my mother and brothers to the railway station at Mukono and shed my bitter tears saying my farewells. They departed for Mombasa and I returned to the empty house in Koja. I felt as miserable as an abandoned orphan. The next day however a sensation of independence and freedom took possession of me. I went to Kampala and saw it with the eyes of an adult. It was a revelation. The town was swarming with Indians; the shops, the banks and the restaurants were all in their hands and the poor Africans were acting like servants. I found a "Bata" shoe shop and bought a pair of sandals. I strolled through the streets of dilapidated wooden shacks and saw the undernourished children with swollen stomachs and bare feet. Then I came across an attractive park near the centre and finished my walk in a splendid cathedral.

Life in Koja continued but with diminished population. Uncle Bronislaw and his family were staying at the hospital until its closure. He planned to settle in Canada afterwards. Two weeks later I received instructions to be ready to go to England with the rest of my family. On the deck of the ship Carnarvon Castle at the Mombasa pier I bumped into my mother. What a wonderful surprise! Presumably my group was added because the ship was under capacity! It was fantastic to be again together. The boat was very different from the one which brought us four years earlier to Africa. It was luxurious!

The ship left the port the very day I had the luck to join it. Walking on the deck I watched Mombasa disappearing in the setting sun and reflected on the events of my four years in Africa. Nostalgically I was thinking about the changing hues of the magnificent lake Victoria, with its silvery waters in the morning changing to deep blue during the day ending with the spectacular reds of the setting sun. During storms it heaved with big waves and lightening vividly lit the surface. At full moon it through back an entrancing sight with innumerable stars glittering in the water. I loved the tropical rain dancing and splashing about in my tennis shoes. I recalled the colonies of flamingos striding on their long legs across the shallow water; the fabulous flora and wildlife. In spite of all that I had no regrets about leaving the black Continent; rather a sense of relief. I wanted badly to return to Europe and I was full of expectations.

The journey started in perfect weather and the sea was calm. We, the girl guides, had various meetings and games, singing and watching the dolphins playing around the ship. Some girls, with flowers in their hair, flirted with the crew while their mothers were relaxed on the deck. I remember the entry to the Red Sea near Aden as one of the hottest places I have ever experienced. Then we passed through the Suez Canal with its contrasting banks of green fields and palm trees on the left and the rocky desert of the Sinai to the right. I felt pretty close to the mysterious St. Catherine monastery. The masts of sunken ships were testimony of the destruction of the war. When we reached Alexandria the climate changed abruptly. The temperature dropped drastically and it became impossible to stand on deck.

It was the end of February and we had no warm clothes. From somewhere some rolls of beige flannel appeared on the ship and a special room was converted into a dress making salon. The ladies were making coats in a hurry – they looked more like overalls. None of my family acquired such a garment. They made these who wore them look like members of the Chinese army, but they helped a great deal when we were passing the Rock of Gibraltar. The Bay of Biscay was very rough and most passengers were sea sick. On approaching Southampton everybody came on deck to welcome the final stage of our wanderings through the world. It had lasted for nearly ten years!

On the way to England

V. A NEW LIFE IN ENGLAND

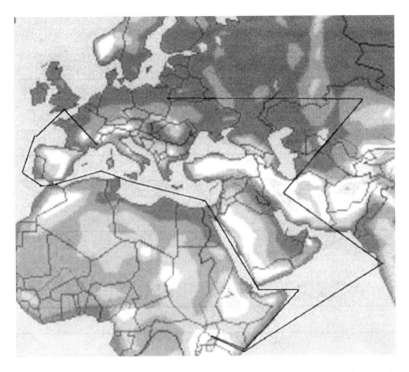

We arrived at Southampton in the late afternoon of 3rd March 1948. The quay was empty and cold, nobody was waiting for us. Holding to the rails and looking down I noticed two Polish soldiers gazing at the boat and I heard the comment. "Look at these kolchoznice (women from kolkhoz farms). Italian girls were much nicer!" In a hurry I found few ladies wearing smart lamb fur coats from Teheran and pushed them forwards in front of beige uniforms. I must say, this first jaundiced encounter dampened my enthusiasm for the heroes of Narvik, Tobruk and Monte Casino.

After disembarkation we travelled by lorries to a camp in Cirencester and were accommodated there in one of the barracks. The night was very cold, but in the morning the sun was shining through the skylights. Inside, our barrack dormitory looked something like a Turner painting: the mist was rising from our beds because the blankets were damp. But breakfast revived us.

Afterwards we were sorted out by various officials who registered us and directed us to one of the barrel shaped metal barracks. There was an atmosphere of uncertainty. I heard a whisper that we were to be sent to various factories in the area. The nearest one to us manufactured china. Fortunately father arrived the following day to give us moral support. I made contact with the scouts and met Rys, an instructor I knew from Teheran and we resumed our scouting activities, excursions and camp fires. Cirencester is a very interesting old town famous for fascinating Roman ruins which abound in the vicinity. For first time in many years I went to a cinema. Then it was decided that I should go to London to contact Scouts headquarters. I eagerly consented.

On a chilly but sunny morning with my small case I arrived at Paddington station, then took the underground to Gloucester Road. Emerging from the station with beating heart I felt like a bird let out of cage. On the pavement a man was playing the violin and touched by his playing and circumstances I dropped half a crown into his cap. My one and only half a crown. I was warmly received at No 49 and a camp bed was given for me to spend the night in the office.

The next morning I busied off to Kensington Gardens in search of Peter Pan's statue. The park was a flood of daffodils and primroses. A flock of sheep was grazing in their midst and I wondered if I was really in London. Then I passed a young woman in high heel shoes with painted seams on her bare legs, the post – war sign of a stocking shortage. Although it was almost three years since war ended, food and many other items were still rationed.

I received my ration, began to learn English, helped in the house, and most enthusiastically of all explored London. Scouts' House was run partly as a hostel so with the few shillings a week earned by cleaning the dormitories I could afford to go skating in Queensway rink. I also went to the opera for the first time in my life. It was Carmen at Covent Garden. Often I just wandered around, visiting such places as Barkers store and Derry and Toms in High Street Kensington with its beautiful roof gardens, Trafalgar Square and the many other famous places in the heart of London.

During the summer I was sent to various refugee camps to welcome and help to settle in the young people arriving from Africa. I also acted as secretary to the Chief of Girl Guides, a truly outstanding person. Twice I went to see the Olympic Games at Wembley Stadium and chanted together with the excited crowd ZA – TO – PEK, the name of the Czech runner who won three gold medals.

The atmosphere in Scout's House was one of great comradeship and when I decided to enrol for a course to study architecture all the instructors were very supportive. One repaired for me an old bicycle rusting in the cellar and another gave me his father's set of drawing instruments. My application for a scholarship at the Polish Committee of Education was refused because I was female civilian and had already been working as a teacher in Africa. My father paid the annual fee for the first year and I continued to live at Gloucester Road.

Cycling to South West Essex College and School of Art in north–east London near Epping Forest took over an hour. But the traffic was easy and I soon became familiar with the route. It was great fun to turn at Hyde Park Corner then at Piccadilly to Holborn, past Sadlers Wells Theatre through Islington to Finsbury Park, a straight run from Manor House to Bell Corner at Walthamstow. Soon on the left appeared the imposing Town Hall building and next to it a neo–classical building in red brick with a stone frieze, colonnaded porch and a flight of steps. This was my college.

The College

The first year of studies was hard. The class was too big with forty students and we had fifteen subjects; some were too difficult for me. A quarter of students were Polish, a few ex–servicemen including an officer from the Polish division that took part in the liberation of Holland, a few from labour camps in Germany, plus Marysia – a general's daughter, and myself, a girl from the jungle. They all had grants. I was the only one without any money. Strangely, it gave me feeling of complete freedom from temptation.

On my way back from college I often changed route and cycled round the city. St. Paul's cathedral was very impressive situated as it was among the ruins of bombed buildings, weeds and shrubs pushed up through the rubble and birds nested there peacefully. A great area of the city was devastated but now bull-dozers were moving the rubble and cranes were working at full throttle. The rebuilding process was well under way. The bridges across the Thames were particularly beautiful. I remember on the south side of Waterloo Bridge a skeleton of twisted metal project-ed into the sky like a dramatic sculpture, and I felt it should never been dismantled, but retained as a powerful reminder of war.

Many times I paused at Cleopatra's Needle and pondered on its past in Egypt. I saluted Boadicea heroically standing by Westminster bridge in chariot. With great excitement I climbed the steps of the Monument, built to commemorate the Great Fire of London in 1666 and from top I admired the roofs below. Then, only the dome of St. Paul's, Big Ben and the spires of mira-culously surviving city churches could be seen above ruins.

One day in winter my bicycle was stolen while I was watch-ing the Royal Couple at St. Paul's. It was a severe blow because I had no means to pay for travel to the college. My only alter-native was to cheat the public transport system improvising stories to bus conductors and devising escape routes at underground stations. Luckily, Wanda came to my rescue. She was studying sociology at S.W.T.C. and suggested that I share her room in Finsbury, and my brother sacrificed half of his grant to cover my expenses. I bought a second hand bicycle and existed mainly on bread, milk, one egg per week and occasional tin of sardines.

The second year at college was much better. I got a grant and found lodgings near the college in a nice semi–detached house. My landlady, Mrs.Rollason, was a young widow with a ten year old son. Her cooking was tasty and I especially enjoyed her Yorkshire pudding. Full board and lodging cost two pounds per week and she gave me a good sandwich for lunch at college.

I was spending weekends with my family, who had moved to London and found a two bedroom flat near Victoria station. The house was old with sagging floors and gas lighting and there was no bathroom, only a water closet on the landing and a water tap in the kitchen. For a full clean–up we had to go to the public bath near Victoria station. I still remember the brown tiled walls and the enormous tubs which were to disappear a few years later. My parents were pleased to find our flat because in the fifties it was very difficult to find accommodation, especially for for-eigners. The usual answer was: "no blacks and no Poles". For this reason a majority of our compatriots in London were buying their own houses with the "demob" money of their fathers and brothers. As my father spent most of his savings on my education he could not follow that pattern. A lawyer, with a very limited knowledge of English, he took a job in factory. A popular employ-ment for Polish ex–servicemen, especially officers, was in hotels and restaurants. They were jokingly called "The Silver Brigade", a poor generation of fighters for freedom.

For me, life was very interesting and I found my studies very absorbing. In order to see a wide range of architecture it was necessary to travel. So, Marysia and I set off on a hiking tour of historic sites in England, seeking out particularly the Gothic cathedrals.

Beginning at Ely, we went to Guilford, Winchester, Salisbury, Wells and Exeter admiring their sublime spires, stained glass windows, flying buttresses and the various forms of vaulting, internal layout and finishing decoration. We found the towns, villages and countryside charming and some of the ancient sites absolutely fabulous. Stonehenge was easily accessible, then without fences or tunnels – and free of charge. The cows were grazing between the magnificent stones. While travelling from place to place we spent many hours waiting for a free lift, often we walked for miles because at that time there were very few cars on the road. Nevertheless, we managed to see quite a number of picturesque places, such as King Arthur's castle in Tintagel, cobbled streets with donkeys in Clovelly and the funicular descending to the sea in Bude.

During the winter break we decided to go for two weeks to Paris. To accumulate sufficient money for this adventure I was cleaning a big house in Knightsbridge, scraping off old paint and preparing walls for redecoration. At St Lazare station in Paris we were met by a student friend who took us to a pre–booked modest hotel near Parc Monceau. To my despair, friends of Marysia's parents arrived to collect her the next day, leaving me alone in a double room I could not afford. So I went to the brother of Rys, Mrusio, who lived in Paris with his wife Stefa. They invited me to stay with them. They were a wonderful couple and it was a great time sharing Christmas festivities with them. From early morning to sun set I walked the streets and boulevards of Paris, with a sketchpad under my arm and a packet of roasted chestnuts for lunch, singing to myself "I love Paris in the morning.......".

One day, sketching in St. Etienne Church, I ran out of paper and went out in search of an art shop. When I went to pay I discovered to my horror that under my arm was only the sketch, but no handbag. Panic stricken I ran back to the church, praying to St. Anthony and all the other saints for help. In the handbag there was not only the money, but also all my documents. On return I found the church full of people at mass. I pushed myself to the first row of people standing behind the pews and looked carefully around. And there, in the middle of a pew was an empty seat with my handbag on it. My mother would say "guardian angels protect the fools". From that moment Paris became even more beautiful.

I was pleasantly surprised to find in different places many associations with Poland. In the middle of Place d'Alma on a huge pedestal stood an impressive statue of the great romantic poet Adam Mickiewicz, pointing towards the north–east to his beloved Litwa. The names of Polish soldiers who fought beside Napoleon were carved on a beautiful arch in the Tullleries. On the island of St. Louis in the middle of the Seine were many houses occupied by Polish emigrants from nineteenth century. The most imposing was Hotel Lambert. There was also an impressive mansion housing the Polish library, with a big collection of historic old books, documents and ancient treasures.

In one of the churches, St. Germain des Pres, I saw a big sarcophagus of Jan Kazimierz, a Polish king of the seventeenth century who after his stormy reign abdicated and left for France. On one of the bridges traversing Seine stands a statue of St. Genevieve, patroness of Paris sculpted by Landowski, who also made the hands of the gigantic statue of Christ, towering over Rio de Janeiro in Brazil. In another church was a huge nineteenth century picture of Holy Mary in an impressive frame illuminated with a poetic strophe in Polish, beseeching her to protect the Polish people in exile. All these discoveries made me feel nostalgic for my country and I was overwhelmed by her strong ties with France. With Marysia I went to museums and art galleries, to the Casino de Paris and to the Comedie Francaise where I saw "Le Malade Imaginnaire" by Moliere, although my French was not altogether up to it. Also we ventured into the well known night club "Oubliette", where I had my first glass of wine. We passed under the Eiffel Tower, climbed hundreds of steps to the top of Notre Dame and Sacre Coeur, made sketches of our favourite sphinx in the Louvre and walked miles along the Seine, changing sides at every bridge.

On leaving the city Paris remained rooted in my heart and mind. The visit was unforgettable. In London college routine once again took over. Our class, reduced by half in the second year, became more friendly. The age of students varied considerably. Besides the older ex–servicemen there were young boys such as small Matton. Brian was brilliant and he knew it. Jim was attractive with his Sherlock Holmes look including the pipe, but he never showed any interest in me. The Polish group focused on Marysia who had many admirers. I was teased for my provincial behaviour, especially by Adam.

So I decided to part with my long plaited hair and went to hairdresser, who after cutting it tried to console me with the loud remark: "Voila, Ingrid Bergman"! The same evening Marysia's mother persuaded me to put on her lipstick. Looking into the mirror I saw a girl like any other in London. Now I felt I had finally left the jungle behind me.

Our tutor took his students to the Victoria and Albert Museum for sketching various classical statues, a poor substitute for the study tours to Greece and Italy organised by other Schools of Architecture. Our college was not recognised by the RIBA so we had to take our intermediate and final exams at the Institute. I was rather pleased because on home ground I felt sometimes embarrassed by my own competitive spirit. I passed both the written and oral of the Intermediate examination without a hiccup and threw myself into the last two years of study with great enthusiasm.

I was still active in scouting and spent lots of time at Gloucester Road headquarters. I enjoyed camping during the summer holidays, but now with rather less enthusiasm as I became interested in a movement called "Miedzy Morze" – "Between the Seas", organised by a group of people belonging to the area between the Baltic and the Black sea. In my imagination this "united" a block of countries in the centre of Europe potentially stabilising peace in the world. I visualised it as a just and thoroughly democratic union. Alas, my vision was shattered when at one meeting I saw a map of the area with Warszawa printed in large block letters. The author of the map, a Pole, explained that it was because it was the most important city. I withdrew from that movement and concentrated on my studies.

During the winter term our tutor organised a trip to Greenwich, taking a boat from Westminster Bridge down to the Zero Meridian. We visited the magnificent Wren Observatory. The view from there down to the river was breathtaking with a splendid white building of the most perfect proportions in the middle of vast slope: Queen Anne's House. It was designed in the first part of the seventeenth century by Inigo Jones for the queen of James I. The house in Palladian style together with Wren's buildings for the Admiralty closer to the river, and his observatory, created a jewel–like architectural complex.

During the last two years at college I moved from Mrs. Rollason to an unfurnished flat in neighbouring Leytonstone which I was sharing with Pamela. She was a brilliant student and one year my senior. Once I heard a fellow student saying "Pamela is so clever she could become Prime Minister"! Well, who knows what could have happened had she not emigrated to Canada.

Furnishing our flat was a great joy to both of us. One night she woke me up shaking my arm. Water was dripping from her hair and she said, smiling: "You told me that the English are very reserved, but look at me, I have been walking with Bill in the rain for hours"! "How romantic" I said feeling a bit envious.

In 1953 I took the final exams. They were not so easy and I had to retake "Hygiene". I had trouble with flows, wind resistance, light etc. My grant had terminated and I returned to my family in Tachbrook street and started job hunting work as an architectural assistant. Dozens of letters were never answered, so I omitted the "Miss" from my name and thus received few invitations for an interview. Still no joy. On two occasions after pressing the appropriate button for the office on the first floor and entering the hall a man standing on the landing cried out "You are a woman! Sorry, save yourself the trouble climbing the stairs". Finally, Mr. Goldfinger, one of London's leading architects, agreed to see some of my sketches in the evening, but I refused to come back and soon afterwards resigned myself to accepting a position of general help in an architect's office in Victoria street, a sort of office boy. Luckily there was a pressure in finishing a project so I was planted behind a drawing board. A year later I passed the Professional Practice exam and was fully qualified, but not being a British subject I could not be a member of the Royal Institute of British Architects. This was very confusing to my employers. A few years later I had to give up my honourable status of Displaced Person and so I applied for British naturalisation at the same time as my husband. Only then I became a member of the RIBA. I remember joking in the office with my colleagues that I was a much better citizen than they, because while they were British by chance I became British by choice. Indeed, I treated my new allegiance to England very seriously and my ties with London very emotionally.

I must mention my personal feelings about adulthood after the first glass of wine in Paris. During the time of the Festival of Britain in 1951, an extremely exciting time to all Londoners,

I met at a dance a handsome man who seemed different from everybody else. To my relief, Stanislaw did not kiss my hand, a banal custom practiced by my compatriots. Was he, I thought, the long awaited Mr. Right? I left the dance quite early because it was a long way to my lodgings. How surprised I was to see Stanislaw the next morning on the doorstep of my landlady's house. He apparently tricked my friends into giving him my address in Walthamstow. The landlady was taken aback as she considered me a career woman who was not interested in men. However Staszek became a frequent visitor. She became quite enchanted by him as he paid much more attention to her or to Marysia, who was then sharing my room, than to me. There would always be a fried chicken on the table when he came at weekends.

Although he was mysteriously secretive, I loved him. To cut a long story short, the wedding was set for 19 March 1954, a day of dispensation in the Catholic Church during lent – St. Joseph's day. However, the night before, Staszek had to be taken to hospital and was operated on for acute appendicitis. I sat at his bedside with the wedding bouquet while our friends were waiting for us at Brompton Oratory. His first outing three weeks later was to the altar and we were finally married.

For the following years we shared the house bought together with my parents, but we were on the outlook for our own. Our salaries in the fifties were not big, but the Permanent Building Society where I was working at the time offered employees an interest free mortgage on condition that the house was no more than twenty five years old. That in turn meant unrealistic price bracket for us.

With Staszek

One day we spotted a sale notice on a very dilapidated property in Streatham. An offer made by my husband over the telephone was accepted, with the mortgage subject to taking out an
insurance policy with Sun & Life. A meeting was arranged in their

office and an amusing story unfolded as Staszek asked me to represent him. I was welcomed by a distinguished looking gentleman who for a quarter an hour described his splendid firm. Then asked: "When we can expect your husband to arrange to conclude the business"? To my astonishment I heard myself saying: "Sorry. But it is I who will apply for the mortgage". "It is absolutely impossible" he replied. "Why?" I asked. "There is no need to explain, it is our policy. No women". "Why"? I asked again and as though being inspired by unknown forces, I embarked on a long speech referring to the feminist movement at the beginning of the twentieth century. Their brave marches, their chaining themselves to the railings and their demand for women's rights. How they achieved the right to votes – a gracious gesture from men – but fifty years on is it still not the same? I declared my belief in English justice to be shattered! The gentleman looked bewildered and asked: "and what if you have children?". "The children belong to both parents, but I will work harder to provide for them". After some further discussion the advisor succumbed to my arguments and admitted that I was so convincing that he telephoned the managing director. As it was lunch time he was not in his office. I interpreted it as an excuse and returned to my Permanent Building Society office doubting the promise of being informed on the director's return. My doubts were dispelled by the telephone upon entering the office: "Madame, your arguments won, when can you come"? My victory was met with disbelief and congratulations by my colleagues. But I have to explain my motivation. During the war my husband was a prisoner in the German concentration camp in Mauthausen, where his health was undermined to such an extent that he was afraid he would not qualify for the compulsory insurance. He was happy for me to deal with securing the mortgage of one thousand pounds. We managed the other eight hundred pounds with our savings and a little loan from friends.

Before signing the policy I had to make a list of all my illnesses, which was quite impressive and then I was taken to a nearby chemist to check my weight. This detail reminded me of a cow being led to the market in pre–war Poland. About six months later we read in the papers that any woman over forty could apply for a mortgage. This gave me a feeling of satisfaction in contributing to the women's cause. The year was 1958. All our free time was spent in making improvements, decoration and furnishing the house. Orange boxes made good kitchen cabinets and long boards on bricks excellent book shelves. The Barker's store in Kensington had great quantities of wild silk and soon our windows were draped with it. The wave of modernisation brought freedom of expression; it was the time of crazy ideas and enthusiastic friendships. Our painter friend Jan and his wife Dinah, who worked in the London branch of Christian Dior, were leading a bohemian life in a big studio at the bottom of a garden at Archway, dreaming of their own house. After one of their parties my husband said jokingly that if their guests (more than two hundred) would lend them a hundred pounds each they could buy a mansion. Dinah jumped at the idea and sent letters to all round. We were asked for the first hundred, but not having the money available Staszek wrote to a friend in Ireland who in turn asked his landlady for the loan. Soon after Dinah collected enough contributions to pay the deposit on a house and to rent an old shop in Portobello Road, where they founded their art shop "The Centaur Gallery". Into our fairly presentable house moved Jarek, a colleague from S.W.T.C. Staszek started an evening course of engineering and I joined an interesting group, Planning Forum, which organised lectures and weekend visits to various new towns around London.

At the time, an excellent lecture was given by a planner upon return from his visit to Russia. The room was filled to the brim including Russian correspondent from TASS. Towards the end

I sprang up with the question: "Have you noticed any deficiencies in the building industry or in agriculture?" quoting my experience in a brick factory and referring to the rotting corn in the fields, because one screw was missing in the harvester. The speaker paused and then remembered one interesting detail. While walking with the town dignitaries along an alley, he noticed a banner stretched overhead calling the workers to produce 120% of bricks. When he questioned the figure, the answer was that 20% was for waste.

After the meeting was closed, the room emptied. Before I reached the door two Russian correspondents cornered me and treated me to an outburst of wounded national pride. They called me a liar, a criminal and threatened me with all of sorts of dire consequences. The older one with a look of Serov, the chief of NKVD, spoke Russian, asking a smartly dressed younger one to translate. I said that it was not necessary as I perfectly understood Russian. I felt amused and quite light hearted. I asked if they knew Siberia and offered to give them some addresses so they could check if the proper well had been built for the Kazakhs, adding that I loved the steppes! They admitted that they have never been beyond the Ural mountains and I told them they did not know the biggest part of their country. To my suggestion of joining a group in the nearby pub where Planning Forum finished their meetings they almost ran away, while I was received with an ovation.

The life of a working woman in England was rather hard with only two weeks holiday a year. So I took a month's break when changing offices. Staszek was not an enthusiast of frequent holidays, saying this was the attitude of people unsatisfied with their situation. Yet, we went skiing to the Austrian Tyrol, borrowing an outfit from Marysia.

Working in Bloomsbury Square I was near the many interesting sites of London. During lunch break I visited museums, galleries, libraries, even enrolled for a lunch hour course in Russian at a college in Red Lion Square. In the Holborn Library I found in a book titled "Forgotten Monuments" two pages devoted to Sobieski, whose grand daughter Clementine married James II and was the mother of Bonnie Prince Charlie, Pretender to the Scottish throne. Intrigued by the possible connection between the Polish king of the seventeenth century and the Scottish throne I read a fascinating story: At the time of Charles II a port governor visited the city docks and noticed a huge case on the deck of one of the boats. When he was told that it was a shipment from Scotland to Poland he ordered it to be opened. To his surprise he saw a magnificent statue of a horseman of impressive features with a figure of a Turk under the horse's hoofs. He called some craftsmen to change Sobieski's face to the face of Charles the second and that of the Turk into Cromwell's, but they forgot to remove the turban. The statue was placed on a big pedestal near the Mansion House and was for years a major attraction in London. Tourists paid less attention to the beautiful monument of King Charles I at the corner of Trafalgar Square than to Cromwell with a turban. From 1883 the statue has stood in the grounds of Newby Hall, Yorkshire, bearing the plate: "Originally King Jan III Sobieski, as a present from the Stuarts of Scotland to Sobieski fighting the Turks".

In summer we were hitch–hiking in France, leaving our old Austin behind. "You have not lived if you do not hitch–hike" was the motto of our friends Dinah and Jan. In the late fifties my husband encouraged me to make a study tour of Italy. I bought a two week unlimited rail travel ticket and set off with great excitement. It was fabulous and I could write another book about it alone, so I shall mention only one amusing episode. I was warned by Staszek of the temperament of Italian men and, being a young blonde he said I may be troubled by them. This what he told me to do. "First show them your wedding ring; second, call the police; and in most desperate situation, tell them that you are Russian". That summer during a European sporting event in Switzerland, Russian women athletes gained several medals and the tribune collapsed under the weight of their "sublime" bodies.

It was not necessary to apply the final tactic until I got to Sicily, where the almond eyed young men were very insistent on providing me with uninvited company. The word "Russian" had a magic effect. They drew back immediately for at least two meters.

After seeing countless marvels of architecture in different parts of Italy I boarded the night train in Milan. An extraordinary thing happened during the return journey. I shared a compartment with a couple of old Italian peasants who were going to visit their son working in France. They offered me their bread, salami and wine, settling themselves on te lower bench. I climbed to one above, putting on all my clothes because it was September and very cold on the bench without blankets. After some time I could not restrain my shivers and chattering teeth. Then the head of the woman appeared. Without a word she instructed me to step down and told me to lay alongside her. Facing the opposite direction. She lifted her ample skirt, took my feet and put them under her armpits, then covered us both with her copious, heavy clothing. All was done in a complete silence. It was unbelievable! My eyes filled with tears, just as they did years back when I was covered with the Persian carpet on my way to Teheran. I thanked God for the existence of such kind people.

At that time I was working at Sir Thomas Bennet's office, contributing to the design of various projects including office blocks, housing, an air terminal, Smithfield market, and some Mormon churches. While designing their Latter Day Saint church I got quite involved and attended some of their functions. Their "Singing mothers" concert filled the Albert Hall. Contrary to general opinion that polygamy was practised among the Mormons I learnt that, following his second vision, only monogamy was permitted by the founder, Joseph Smith.

VI. ANDREW'S CHILDHOOD

One Monday morning, in January 1963, our son Andrew sprang like a dolphin into the world and became the centre of our life. He was a wonderful baby, but very demanding and his father did not like to hear him crying, so I had a lot of sleepless nights. Once I was rung by one of my scouting comrades, now an eminent professor of psychology in the States, who was passing through London. Hearing Andrew crying in the garden I asked what was his explanation for the child's tears? When he said that it maybe caused by underfeeding, overfeeding, or wanting mother's love, I ran to my baby. All the propaganda against "spoiling" the children seemed to me to be false, and I rather agreed with the theory comparing maternal love with a woman who could be never over loved.

Even before Andrew was born Staszek investigated the question of boy's education. He discussed it with the local priest and with our MP and came to the conclusion that for the boy it would be Harrow School, Westminster School or Dulwich College. A girl should go to the Lycee Francaise. So, at the age of three

Andrew was enrolled at the nursery of Dulwich College after passing the entrance exam with the help of the head master, Mr. Woodcock.

Years went by like a dream. Suddenly our house seemed too small so we decided to move to a bigger one. We found a large, rambling Victorian house with a nice garden behind a tall brick wall which separated it from the street, with a garage at the bottom. The garden was neglected and we had to make a bonfire of the weeds in the spring. Little Andrew, interested in everything, put his hand into the hot cinders. He had a shock and blisters on his hand.

I used to take him to a nearby play group, but he was somewhat withdrawn at the beginning and not keen on sharing his toys. On the first day at the nursery school he did not want me to leave and cried bitterly. But the teacher took him by his hand and very soon I could hear "Yes Mrs. Disher". For some time he was speaking with Mrs. Disher's accent, so all was well. As a small child he was friendly with all the men who visited us, but not with women. When we travelled with a lot of luggage he objected strongly to anyone offering help with our cases. "Do not touch them, they are my mummy's".

Aged three he had trouble with his tonsils. The doctor advised an immediate operation or a change of climate. Staszek decided on the latter and arranged for us to go to Zakopane, the popular tourist centre in the Tatra mountains in southern Poland. We stayed with friends, both architects, and their son Jasio, the same age as Andrew, in an old chalet type house on the outskirts of the town, with magnificent view of the mountains. From the handsome veranda with beautiful wooden carvings, the view stretched over the meadows, now under a blanket of snow, across the black line of pine forest with white caps, towered by the mountain in the shape of a sleeping night – The Giewont. It was easy to be charmed by the magic of the place and I have remained under its spell ever since.

Along the house ran a path as well as a cascading stream. All around us were relics of local architecture – ancient wooden barns built of logs and pitched roofs with shingles.

There were also a number of smart villas built between the wars, with mansard roofs and well proportioned facades. The upper levels were built of pine or cedar logs which rested on a stone masonry base. They were executed by local builders which imparted to them elements of local artistic patterns.

Gubalowka's gentle slopes were favoured by skiers and were easily reached by the funicular railway. The ridge, several kilometres long, was especially beautiful at sunset. When walking into the sun one saw Giewont and the other peaks inflamed with a red glow.

Droga do Daniela

In the valley was Zakopane, and to the right were hilltops covered with forests whose colour turned blue. A procession of sledges with tourists, pulled by horses with ringing bells, added a picturesque touch to the scenery. At the top station there was a man parading in a bear skin, his sledges pulled by two big Husky dogs, offering a backdrop to photos. As Andrew recovered, of course he had to follow the custom.

The people of Zakopane, known as Gorale, were as colourful as their surroundings. Their walk was light and springy, like that of chamois, their voices strong, melodious and vibrating. Their profiles had something of the mountain eagle or American Indian. They wore richly embroidered costumes. A man's outfit was a black felt hat with a band of small sea shells, a short embroidered sheepskin coat over a white linen shirt with a special heart shaped broach, very distinct thick felt trousers, ingeniously embroidered. Women had colourful scarves on their heads with silky fringes and rows of coral and amber beads around their neck. Their blouses had laced collars and they wore brightly coloured and richly sequined corsages and an apron over a printed skirt. When they were singing in chorus the glass in the windows shook.

During Andrew's illness, Wladyslaw, an old Goral, who was helping in our friends' household, had a great influence upon us. Although illiterate he was a visionary man, a man of wisdom. He was nursing little Andrew, who obeyed Wladyslaw unquestioningly, and I had to follow his instructions. He said: "This child comes from an island, so his heart and lungs are small – remember then to bring him gradually to the fresh mountain air. The first time for three minutes only, then five, then ten". That man was a treasure and we loved him. He used to ask me for few zloty to go to the cinema when a Western was showing. He considered the Indians as his brothers. He did not respect the political system nor the state boundaries and often wandered on the southern slopes of the Tatras, putting a feather in his hat, just like the Slovaks. He ignored the rule of compulsory registration and when called to do so at the office exclaimed: "Everybody in the area knows me well enough without any registration, so it is not necessary for me to do it. Only you a newcomer, needs it". Once he asked me if we had a garage in London and when I nodded he proposed to come to visit us one day. He would swim the Channel, than kill a pig for Christmas in the garage, as it is done in the mountains, and make for us a winter supply of hams and sausages. So much of Wladyslaw. Of course there were many wonderful features of the highlands and we went there whenever possible. We adored their customs and Andrew picked their accent. He also befriended Jasio and they became friends for life, playing and learning to ski together.

Our first Christmas among the Highlanders had for me an unreal feeling, it was like a fable. With the first star on a darkening sky on Christmas Eve the whole family of our guests gathered round the table and braking a wafer thin oplatek began exchanging wishes and kisses. The table looked festive with masses of various traditional dishes of fish, salads, dumplings, mushroom soup and a desert of nuts and poppy seeds steeped in honey. Dining was followed by singing beautiful local carols by the candle lit Christmas tree laden with home made decorations. The ceremony of distributing presents took place in a big hall with the fire burning in an enormous stone fire place. Christmas decorations were suspended from the panelled ceiling over the two storey space, with its wide wooden staircase along one wall.

Before midnight our boys were put to bed under the care of Jasio's grandmother, while the hosts and some guests went to the midnight mass called Pasterka in the celebrated old church in Strazyska. For me it was pleasant, with the snow crackling under our feet, and sparkling in the light of rising moon. We joined a crowd of Gazdas and Gazdzinas in their festive costumes and I tried to sing with them, feeling light and airy under the falling snow flakes. The atmosphere was full of emotion as though in the presence of God.

On return I joined Andrew in our tiny room by the gallery, but before I fell asleep the door suddenly opened and a shower of grain fell over us, accompanied by the Highlander's greeting "Na szczescie, na zdrowie, na to Boze Narodzenie!". – "Happiness and health on the day of our Lord's son birth!" It was Jon Marusarz, most senior gazda in the Tatra and the father of an Olympic champion of the thirties. I had the impression nobody did sleep that night in Zakopane.

The following year I joined a group of young Highlanders and after Pasterka we wandered from house to house making short cuts in the deep snow, singing, drinking and dancing till dawn, then taking skis and children to the slopes.

The winter breaks in the Tatra mountains had a magic charm and continued for the next few years, until Andrew joined the Kandahar Ski Club in England.

When he was ten years old he and the other boys in the Preparatory school had to prepare a major portfolio on a specific subject. Andrew received a long list of questions under the title "Poland". It was rather hard on him because at home he was spared any political or religious "isms" and his contact with Poland was limited to Highlanders environment. As Krakow, the ancient capital of Poland was only a hundred kilometres from Zakopane we took a bus there in order to show Andrew some historic sights and to take photographs. After leaving King Zygmunt's chapel in Wawel castle he asked me thoughtfully: "Do people in England have knowledge of this chapel? I have never seen anything so beautiful".

The most impressive and bewildering experience were the salt mines of Wieliczka, near Krakow. The site is of a wonder beyond description. Entering the enormous underground void I exclaimed "Pyramids", to a great disapproval of one of salt mine's guardians. "It is salt, not stone" he corrected me. We found ourselves in the world of magic, walking along corridors constructed with thousands of big timber logs. Spacious chambers of fantastic shapes, some on a scale of a Gothic cathedrals.

Some were approached by a flight of stairs, others surrounded by a lake. All the walls and vaulting were textured with the carvings done by ancient workers who had worked exclusively in the salty rocks. Most of the enormous spaces contained religious statues, but some were of political figures of communist Poland, something to which I strongly objected. There were also rooms, which were transformed centuries ago into chapels full of effigies of saints, whose features have mellowed by a formation of salty crust. They looked mysterious, these old companions, who watched the hard working miners crouched on scaffolds, digging for the priceless mineral. The lower level of the mine was turned into a sanatorium for treating pulmonary problems, especially asthma. In another part was a museum.

I stopped in astonishment in front of one showcase, seeing the word "Pyramids". A French traveller in sixteenth century had a reaction identical to mine. Only his comment read "They were not for the glory of Pharaoh but for the welfare of people". Few years later I was very pleased to find in a book entitled "Architecture without architects" a whole page devoted to Wieliczka.

Andrew was so impressed by the mine that the next week we revisited it, bringing Jasio and his father. After spending most of the afternoon in this fabulous place we were full of excitement on the way to Zakopane, when near Myslenice Jasio's father car broke down. All his vigorous attempts to revive the engine were fruitless and we had to abandon the vehicle and go to the nearest bus stop. It was getting very cold. Waiting for the bus with the sinking sun behind the peaks of the Tatra with the temperature dropping below zero seemed to be endless. Somehow we managed to get home.

Occasionally my husband, Staszek, although not a Goral, where this name was exceptionally popular, joined us towards the end of the holiday. He was a great supporter and protector of our boys. He watched them on the slopes and cooled down the angry adult skiers who were outmanoeuvred by our youngsters at the head of the lift queue by saying: "You have no chance of becoming an Olympic champion against these boys, so let them pass!".

Andrew and Jasio

Jasio was a born skier and at the age of ten he joined a racing team under the care of a trainer who trained them all year round along with their academic studies. Andrew was very sad to loose his companion on the slopes. But eventually he was accepted as an extra during his winter holidays. At the beginning he lagged behind but after few days he reached the required level. The instructor tried to convince me to leave Andrew for a year in his hands because he said: "Andrew has in him all that is required to became a skiing champion – well balanced physique and psyche". To my question about school his answer was that Andrew could pick it up later, and anyhow "Look at the Gross brothers, Italian Olympic champions, I don't think they went to school past elementary stage". I just laughed, trying to imagine my husband's reaction.

Andrew skiing

Later he advised Andrew to stop going to winter holidays with his mother, and join a ski club in England. So, after some investigation, he became member of the Kandahar Ski Racing Club. The following winter I went to Courmayeur to watch him racing in the European "under sixteen" competition. The boys looked wonderful in that sunny, frosty afternoon. Andrew was thirtieth and his trainer told me that if he had been with him from the age of eleven he could easily become an Olympic champion. But he decided not to continue and withdrew from the Racing Club, though remained an active skier throughout his school and university career.

In December1981 during the tragic events in Poland, Jasio was training for the Olympics in Austria and being unable to spend Christmas with his family in Zakopane, he telephoned us in London to request the necessary invitation and visa before joining us for a few days. I spent whole day of 23rd of December in Home Office in Croydon begging officials for the visa, but faced cold, impersonal reaction to my request. While in many houses in Europe candles were lit in sympathy for the Polish Solidarity, the English bureaucracy stopped the issue of visas. In a dry voice the clerk said: "Anyway the boy will have a nice Christmas in Austria". Our disappointment was immense. A few days later Andrew went to meet him in Schladming in Austria, to cheer him up and to ski for a while together.

Jasio did not go back to Poland that winter and after receiving a USA visa he studied and skied for the University of Salt Lake City. He developed a great passion for cross country cycling. In recent years he brought to perfection a mountain bike, designing, constructing and demonstrating his own model, "The Karpiel".

Beside skiing, Zakopane offered other attractions. Clubs, bars and restaurants were always full, as were the theatre, cinema and some art galleries. Our hosts introduced us to the local artists, who resided permanently in Zakopane but nevertheless gained national reputation in the country, and occasionally abroad.

The most talked about at the time were Hasior and Rzasa. The first was a truly modern artist, expressing his inner ego in powerful outbursts of flames, light, water, barbed wire, knife blades, candles, music in the wind and much else. His studio was surrounded by enormous images on ecclesiastical–like banners. He created his masterpieces mainly from resurrected treasures from rubbish dumps, even using loaves of bread. I was caught up in his spell and intended to organize an exhibition of his work in London. Negotiations with one of the art galleries of South Kensington went ahead, but unfortunately Hasior withdrew at the last moment because he had to cover the cost of transport to Dover himself before the London gallery would take over.

Antoni Rzasa was my "Michelangelo" in wood. His figures of Christ, angels, children and animals were captivating in their excellence and finesse. He lived with his wife and son in a large room–cum–studio, with a baby cradle made by him in the middle surrounded by his beautiful carvings, which projected from the walls and threw mysterious shadows. They lived very modestly but he would not part with his work for any price.

After befriending him I had a good fortune to receive from him a piece he made for his baby boy in return for a set of carving chisels from London. I took to Antoni's studio my friend Alexandra from Rio de Janeiro, who burst into tears of emotion when she entered. "Ask him if he would like to come to Brazil?" she said with the conviction that she had met a great artist, and a visionary man.

Both these artists, years after living in their small, crowded, but very charming studios were later allocated spacious houses, specially built for them. However, the new surroundings did not make the same visual and emotional impact. Maybe it takes time for the artistic spirit to create strong ties with surroundings.

In the house of our hosts Staszek and Madzia, a middle class girl from Krakow, there was always a large crowd of friends from many parts of Europe. We met there artists, writers and travellers like Izabella and Janusz, the Norwegian journalist Douglas, painters and actors. Siri was a very colourful Norwegian person who secured a scholarship for postgraduate study of weaving with the celebrated Abakunowicz in Krakov. She was spending her weekends skiing and was staying for the night with Staszek and Madzia. So Saturday nights were full of Goral's music and dances. Siri demonstrated a special way of eating fish as taught by her mother, an authority on healthy diet in Norway and a writer on this subject. To Andrew and Jasio's amusement Siri consumed the entire cooked fish from head to tail, bones, skin and the rest, proving her mother's theory that this was the best way to keep ones teeth white and strong.

The atmosphere in the house was too bohemian for my husband who could not even tolerate cigarette smoke, so Staszek decided to buy his own place. He approached Jon Marusarz for advice. Jon sent his niece Hanka to look for a simple "Goralska Chata" (typical local house), and one was found in Blachowka, on the slopes of Gubalowka, high above the valley of Zakopane with a breathtaking view of the Tatra range. It was a small house laid out for a farmer's family and their animals. The smell of animals was still noticeable. It was built from sizeable pine logs with a pitched roof with cedar shingles. Underneath the roof was an enormous loft with openings each end for bringing in the hay for winter storage. The loft could be reached from inside on a peg like ladder, giving Andrew plenty of climbing enjoyment.

We found ourselves in the middle of a rural community with smallholdings scattered on the slopes of Gubalowka. I was eager to make contacts with our new neighbours. The nearest was Anna, mother of the previous owner of our house. A slim, elderly woman, who spoke with a very strong local accent, she lived with twin sons in a spacious house, which they partly turned into a hostel. Her personal habitat was less than modest, with her bed in the kitchen and her belongings hanging above it next to the holy pictures on the wall. She worked hard on her smallholding and supplied us with milk and eggs. She also helped me start the fire in the kitchen stove, which was very old and smoked a lot. We got the water from a well a few yards up the slope. The toilet was outside the house and offered the best view of Gievont, especially in the rising sun across the valley with Zakopane below under a thick blanket of morning mist.

On the other side was a prosperous farm with several domestic animals and quite a big carpentry workshop. The family had nearly a dozen children, mostly lovely girls. They helped me to organize a house warming party, turning it into quite a big event.

The twins prepared the house by throwing most of furniture into the snow outside the windows and turned the "boisko" previously occupied by the animals into a well equipped bar.

Vodka was abundant. The house was filled with people to the magic sound of "goralska muzyka". I was enchanted to see Gorals happily entertaining guests from town.

Jon Marusarz, a sick man, was treated with great respect and admiration because he bravely decided to join the party in spite of his advanced illness. As the house could be reached only across a steep wooded slope, he was carried on the shoulders of young men.

The night passed quickly with dancing, singing and drinking. The twins who served the drinks sobered themselves up by rolling in the snow from time to time. All the guests were very merry and only calmed down towards the morning.

During the following winters in Blachowka Andrew often preferred to stay with Jasio in town and they skied and enjoyed the company of other youths.

In London our life consisted of synchronising work and the school time table. Staszek arranged with his employers Arup and Partners to have shorter hours in order to collect Andrew from school at 3pm while I was working full time to 5.30 in Lambeth. Staszek catered for the summer school holidays and I for the winter and the spring ones.

During long weekends and half term breaks we made several excursions and visited many historic places which gave me a lot of pleasure.

Going back to Andrew's school project, it was well presented and he obtained a high mark. We were extremely pleased with discovering Wieliczka and spread its fame whenever we could. The last time Andrew went to Zakopane was in 1990 when he brought the ashes of his father to be buried in the family grave in Sokolow Podlaski. Then he came to the mountains for one day only, revisited familiar places and said goodbye to the Tatra mountains.

House on Blachowka

VII. DOOZES

Early in 1970 we were intrigued by an announcement in the Sunday Observer which reported the formation of Wadhurst Park and Leisure Centre. We knew the area well from many weekends spent there in 1950. It was beyond our understanding that this beautiful unspoilt and isolated corner of Sussex should be invaded by crowds of city people with their consuming appetites. We attended the meeting, joined the Syndicate, paid our share of two hundred and fifty pounds, and decided to revisit Wadhurst.

The big estate consisted of a partly ruined manor. Coombe Farm and Doozes Cottage belonged to a few demobilized Polish officers. Over the years the majority of them departed, finding it too difficult to metamorphose from pre–war landlords to hard working farmers. Only one owner of Coombe, Kostek, remained and made it a successful farm. We joined him in the fields where on his tractor he was spreading fertiliser over the area. We were pleased he recognised us after so many years. He has remarried and lives in a beautiful house with his young family. He recollected the happenings of the past decade and told us that part of the main estate was up for sale and also said that, shortly, Doozes Cottage will be for sale, too. Apparently there were prospective buyers for it, but they were hesitant because it was thought that the cottage was haunted. The Syndicate was shortly dissolved due to the strong opposition of the neighbouring rural community.

A few days later we received a phone call from Kostek telling us that the potential buyer of Doozes had withdrawn so we jumped at it. Without even a visit the sale was completed over the telephone. The XVI century relic and four and half acres of land became ours.

The cottage was uninhabitable but it looked charming, with roses embracing the walls and entering the house through broken windows. The high grass with giant nettles (excellent for soups and salads), wild flowers, forget–me–nots, marguerites, violets and most of the flowering weeds surrounded the house. There was a row of old apple trees and the site was bordered by a thick growth of thorny bushes. On one side was a dense forest. Many magnificent trees – huge beaches, walnuts, birches and firs flourished their ancient roots dating back to the time of the charcoal industry.

There were three hammer–head ponds with man–made mounds between them, the remains of 7th and 8th centuries iron–ore mining. Later on Doozes became a cider farm and a smallholding. It was finally abandoned after the First World War, the farmer having lost his life on the front.

The other side was open to the wide horizon, offering an unrestricted view of rolling fields and meadows with the occasional tree, but not a house in sight. The feeling of space was uplifting and Staszek and I were captivated by it. Andrew enjoyed climbing trees and chasing pheasants. The focal point was an enormous oak in the middle of a clearing which we were told dated from William the Conqueror.

In the past a country lane boarded by oak trees on one side and a beech fence on the other linked the cottage with the neighbouring villages. Now it terminated within the site boundary merging into meadow. It was water–logged in places and it was not suitable for motor cars .The only access was a right of way over a rough ground through Wadhurst Park.

We applied to the Council for permission to rebuild the cottage, or to build a new one next to it. Luckily Staszek found a way to obtain permission for repairs. I made the necessary drawings and agreed with the council the choice of materials and invited the local builders to estimate. Unfortunately, on his first visit it started raining heavily, the ground became soggy and it took the unfortunate builder a few hours to reach solid ground, even after using branches of trees and parts of his clothes under the wheels of his car. In consequence we never heard any more from him, nor from any of the others either.

Aerial view of Doozes

A glimpse of hope came when Kostek decided to build a farm house near his dairy for his son. He was pleased with my design of the house but horrified by the cost quoted by the builders. So, after lengthy discussions, we risked building both houses ourselves with a workforce imported from the Tatra mountains. Kostek agreed to transport all the materials needed for Doozes across the fields by tractor and it was up to me to negotiate with the Gorals when I next visited Poland for skiing.

Things were moving. The next summer four Gorals, builders from Zakopane, arrived as our guests, as did my cousin, a shipping engineer from Gdansk, who became a general helper and cook on the site. They were accommodated in Coombe farm partly in a farmer's cottage and partly in a caravan.

The weather was fine and spirits high. After a few days of acclimatization and trips to various building sites they were ready to show their skills. Their soft spot was bricklaying, because they were used to building with stone and timber with which they were true artists.

We also visited some historic sites and I was favourably impressed by their response to various details of Elizabethan architecture. Towards the end of the summer the Kostek's house was almost finished and we celebrated topping of the roof. On the way to Coombe for celebrations I met by chance at the greengrocer's shop our old friend Siri, the Norwegian whom we knew in Zakopane a few years earlier. She was in that shop by chance on her way to a party, but of course she landed with us as Staszek liked her very much.

The Gorals, who used to play and sing to her in Zakopane, were flabbergasted to see her and rejoiced. Andrew remembered her spectacular show of eating a whole fish, and asked for a repeat performance of it in London when she visited us while lecturing at the London School of Art. Soon after she returned to Norway.

With Kostek's house under roof, came the turn of Doozes with gorals arriving every morning in an old Land Rover. The first visit of the building inspector was alarming. He saw the roof (whatever was left of it) was supported only by a leaning post with an enormous chimney standing in the middle of the empty floor. The Gorals gesticulated to convey that the collapse of the walls and roof was imminent. It turned out that conservation of the old cottage was out of the question. The restoration could be carried out by using new materials but retaining the character, proportions, and detail as near as possible to the original. Staszek had a marvellous rapport with Gorals and they did everything to please him. But they treated me with reservation and bare tolerance.

We had to cater for the team so each weekend we brought a car full of provisions. With the autumn rain it became impossible to reach the house by car so it was necessary to travel half of the way, about a kilometre, on foot. It was amusing to see us loaded with rucksacks and large pressure cookers of cooked meals, sliding on the muddy path.

The Oak Tree

A few times it was necessary to handle a window frame left by the delivery van because the driver could not get any closer. The huge roof over two floors on one side was constructed in the original manner without a nail or screw, with all joints and locks beautifully in place. During the visits of the building surveyor communication proceeded by deaf and dumb gestures and at critical moments the Gorals telephoned us asking for help because "the surveyor turned red in the face". This was generally when "British Standards" were invoked, while the Gorals tended to apply own rules of common sense. For example, instead of lead flashing they applied cement. On the whole, things were going well and Goral's songs echoed in the countryside. At weekends we had huge camp fires, with dances, baked potatoes and sausages.

Before Christmas our guest builders left for their homes and their families. Doozes remained unfinished. In spring Staszek engaged casual labour and most of the work was completed. We and our friends would soon have the pleasure of spending weekends at the cottage – while clearing the site of building debris. Many times I turned to the invisible ghost asking him to lend a hand with the hard work, but of no avail. Though some people swore they saw a tall figure with golden spectacles, huge sombrero hat and black cape down to the ground.

One sunny Sunday we had a visit by an elderly lady with her son, an archaeologist from York. They stopped and expressed joy at finding the house. They were on a quest for their ancestors with a detailed map of the region. It appeared that Doozes was mentioned in a marriage settlement of 1666 giving Ann, the daughter of Thomas Manser, gentleman, 50 acres of land called Doozes. Thus we got to know a bit more about its past. It was an interesting meeting and many parts of the site were classified professionally.

In parallel with the restoration of the cottage, a great restoration appeared at the neighbouring Wadhurst Park which, after some changes of ownership became an impressive deer park with hundreds of deer, including the Manchurian breed uncommon in Europe.

The Deer

This new thousand acres sanctuary surrounded Doozes from almost three sides by a three meter high wire net fences, with a few gates providing right–of–way to our cottage. Driving through we were restrained so as not to disturb the animals.

It was delightful to watch the herd of young ones performing their antics in front of our car. The big Asiatic ones somewhat resembled camels. When sometimes caught by surprise they gave a hair raising show of turning their heads with enormous antlers on top and pawing the ground furiously with their hind legs. At the same time they were arching their tails and puffing steam with a whistling noise. It was spectacular!

Staszek had a gift for starting friendships and soon knew the neighbours. He bought another right–of–way in the opposite direction, which years later Andrew turned into a proper road with a view to establishing there a permanent home for his young family. A few years later he obtained the building permission. But at what price? The existing house had to be demolished as the permit allowed only the new one on the site. I was devastated. Nothing is left of our charming nook that both my husband and I cherished so much – except memories and photos. But a new house has risen in its place.

Doozes Cottage – the old and new.

VIII. DISCOVERING PROVENCE

Besides our preoccupation with the house and garden and my sporadic work on the drawing board for my friend Pamela in my early retirement, I was preparing plans for rebuilding a ruin in the South of France. I was on the way to Sunshine. To get to the point, I have to go back to Andrew's childhood. We were told by his teacher in the Nursery that it was essential to accustom him to water, as he got out of the swimming pool with dry pants. This simply had to change as next year boys would be taken to the Crystal Palace swimming pool.

So Staszek decided to take him to the Mediterranean Sea. He bought a tent and camping equipment and set up camp at Port Grimaud on the French coast. A few days later I received a telegram: "Come and take over, I am dying". I was, of course very worried and uncertain what to do. The following day another telegram arrived with instructions to take the train to Les Arc. I arranged emergency leave from the office and with trembling heart set off to my unknown destination. At Les Arc my husband was waiting with a broad smile, looking very well. He explained the cause of his alarm. When camping by the sea he felt as though dying from a heart attack and was in great pain. So he decided to take Andrew to some people in Callian whose address he had from my friend Isabelle. Just before arriving at the square – la place du Chateau where friends of Isabelle had their studio, called Venona – Andrew fell sick, so he was put to bed with the cats and dogs of the hosts and Staszek was instructed to go and bring the camping stuff. He was in agony yet he erected the tent on the grounds of the tiny cottage of Jolanda and Wlad on the outskirts of the village. To his great relief the next morning his heart was beating normally and he felt no more pain. A miracle he thought, and chuckled when he heard that the area was known for its cardiac benefits.

It was too late to cancel the telegram of course, so we enjoyed a week together. The area was fabulous, with the Litoral Alps rising to the north and Massif du Esterel to the south. The air was saturated with the scent of the herbs of Provence: thyme, rosemary, sariette, marjoram and many others. The azure sky was slightly powdered by the intensity of the sun. For the purest azure one has to be here in the winter, we were told by Wlad.

Next door to our friends was a farm with its peach orchard reaching the fence. Naturally, Staszek made friends with the farmer and soon we were having mountains of peaches for breakfast.

The main attraction of the area was Lac de St. Cassien, formed artificially some twenty years earlier after the burst of a dam near Frejus. Andrew finally learned to swim and for me it was paradise equal to Lake Victoria – but without the bilharzias.

Lake St. Cassien

For the next few years our summer holidays were spent by the lake, with my husband driving down at the beginning of school holidays and me replacing him two weeks later, arriving by train to Cannes. After a day on the beach, Staszek took the train with my return ticket to London and I drove with Andrew to Callian. Staszek, with his gift for making friends, met charming mothers and their children at the lake and Andrew started to learn French. Following the activities of Staszek I received invitations from various local people. The first one was truly memorable. It was for lunch at the house of a retired colonel. I was taken by the over elaborate etiquette with which he treated me but he commented: "I am paying the debt of Napoleon", an unofficial legacy the Emperor left to high ranking officers of his army. He assured me I would feel at home in France: it reminded me of a book I read in my childhood entitled "The two patrimonies", referring to France and Poland. The colonel became our friend during our first visits to Callian. He helped us to put roots in the rocky ground but unfortunately he died a few years later.

Our hosts Jolanda and Wlad were extremely colourful figures. She painted naive pictures incorporating images of cats with ladders and fountains in foreground. She was a writer and taught French to newcomers from Africa. She was a general advisor on any of the day to day problems. Her posture was commanding, her looks authoritarian.

Wlad was strikingly different; small, skinny, and almost bald. He was running a photographic studio next to his wife's atelier, all within the Callian castle forecourt. In the evening they returned to their home "Venona" where we often shared dinner and listened to Jolanda's tales before and after the First World War. She was a kind of French suffragette and very active in the film world of the Twenties.

Staszek was rather sceptical with regard to the truthfulness of her stories, but I was totally taken by them. Her way of life was unorthodox and their house was unusual. The walls and all the furniture was covered with colourful images of abstract floral forms. The floor was occasionally swept with a broom held by her toes because – due to numerous cancer operations to her stomach – she was unable to bend easily. Her culinary skills were extraordinary and very original, like her poetry.

One of her friends was Christian Dior, who lived in neighbouring Montauroux. According to her, the famous New Look created by him in the fifties was for her, to cover the varicose veins which disturbed her. She claimed to know Georges Clemenceau, one of the architects of the Treaty of Versailles in 1918. After the fabulous years in Paris Jolanda came to Provence with her husband to live simply in this modest "bergerie", a gift from a lesbian friend of the thirties.

The couple existed on an absolute minimum income since Wlad never obtained the necessary demobilization papers from the R.A.F. The photo studio was not very profitable and what was left after the rent was spent on their beloved pets. Jolanda had discovered her passion for painting earlier on in Paris, where she earned a living from grooming cats and dogs in their luxurious apartment. Now in Provence she took part in various art exhibitions held during the summer along the Mediterranean coast and I often enjoyed driving her with her paintings.

In Venona a pleasant harmony prevailed between our hosts and the "boys". Jolanda marked out the outline of foundations for a house for us in the corner of her "prairie". She adored Staszek's courteous attentions and gladly paraded on his arm throughout the grounds of the village during its "fete" and made him to invite her to dance. But it did not last for ever. In the summer of 1972 my husband telephoned me from Callian asking me to come two days earlier.

He could no longer bear the hospitality of Venona and Jolanda's capricious temper. He decided we must have something of our own in this wonderful locality. I was not surprised. There were frequent occasions in our house in London when Staszek, after weeks of charming hospitality on his part, brought tears to the eyes of many lady guests when he became transformed into an impolite macho.

The builder working on the roof of Venona took us on a day trip to look at some sites and houses but nothing appealed to us until we came to the ruins of a Bergerie – a sheep barn in the woods of the rising slopes above the village of Callian. It was so picturesque that I started dancing among the trees intoxicated with the beauty of the surroundings. The next day my husband returned to London and over the telephone bought the ruins, arranging payments through our friends on the Continent because there were restrictions on taking large amounts of money from England.

The Ruins

The Bergerie was charming but it was so overgrown that we could not even erect a tent there, so we continued to camp at Venona. Early morning before breakfast I went there to spend some time clearing the site to make a patch for the tent. In the meantime we shared life with Jolanda and Wlad, swimming in the lake almost daily and making excursions. Jolanda's pictures began to sell like hotcakes, specially in the gallery of Juliette in Flayosc, where she was feeding the local clientele in a tastefully arranged restaurant on the ground floor, and then directing them to the exhibition rooms on the upper levels. She was very successful in selling her collection but she never paid Jolanda, which I did not understand until I became aware of their lesbian friendship.

Juliette was regularly delivering painting materials to the studio of Jolanda, leaving it with an armful of "primitives". Her life came to a sad end when cancer took final hold on Jolanda and on one of our visits we found her in Grasse hospital. She was still a fighter and very much alert.

On my several visits with her mail, she asked me to read her letters in Polish, waiting impatiently for some information from the Wawel Castle Museum in Krakow. She had sent for verification a photograph of some old armour believing it to be a fourteenth century item of King Louis the Great of Hungary, who was also King of Poland. The armour is now in the museum of Draguignan.

When the answer did arrive she was very disappointed to learn that it was an ornamental copy of the eighteenth century. I heard her whisper "Oh Poles, they are only experts in sausages and vodka". Not very tactful, I thought. She had been desperate to find historical truth in the myth of Louis. It was said that Louis came to Provence to seek revenge for the death of his brother Andrew in Naples. He came as far as Draguignan in pursuit of Andrew's widow, the beautiful Joanne, queen of Jeruzalem and Naples, and Grande Duchesse of Provence, who was travelling to Avignon to ask the Pope's forgiveness.

The story goes that when he heard there was a plague near Dragiugnan he dropped his armour and ran away in his underwear. Jolanda was sure that the piece of armour was Louis's. Wlad took a photograph of it and sent it to the Polish museum. Alas, it was not what she believed it to be. She died shortly after this episode. Wlad brought us the sad news, followed by Juliette who was consoling him. Soon after came the mayor of the village with his wife to pay their condolences to an old friend. They took me aside and asked if I could help to liberate Wlad from the strange power Juliette held over him. Andrew was listening and remarked spontaneously: "She is like somebody who takes the last penny from a blind's man box". This proved to be prophetic as in few years she took possession of the whole of Venona, proving in court that for years she had supported the couple. She successfully disposed of her rival Dorothy, a gifted painter who for years had occupied a little annex of Venona and, after the death of Jolanda, considered herself the rightful owner. It was a very sad time for Wlad, who also suffered from Parkinson disease.

On one visit from London we had a real shock when we found him in an empty room, moaning on an a narrow dirty bed in the middle of dirty floor covered with vermin. With tears in his eyes he asked us to bring back his big matrimonial bed from Jolanda's studio if Dorothy had not taken it with their other possessions to London. Andrew was a great help in getting the bed through the window and recovering some broken pieces of furniture.

Wlad had a local nurse visiting him twice a week but he needed a constant supervision. With his trembling hands he could not hold a glass of water let alone cook his meals. A few months later Dorothy managed to place him in hospital, cleared the house completely and disappeared. The house was intended to be an Art Gallery and a museum of Jolanda but after Wlad's death in the late seventies Juliette sold it. Only a little board bears the name of Jolanda.

Some years later Staszek and myself made a trip to Flayosc, determined to find Juliette. We did find her but she was almost unrecognisable, looking poor and ill, with none of her previous glamour. But part of her house was devoted to Jolanda, almost as a shrine. She admired her very much and wanted to write a book about her, but I believe she never managed it.

When our site became more accessible we began to camp there and made a cooking area in the ruins.

Reconstruction of Bergerie

Our bathroom was the lake – some ten kilometres away. We always equipped ourselves with bowls and buckets in order not to pollute the lake with soap. It was great fun but it did not last long. One day upon returning from the lake we found a couple of policemen waiting for us. They forbade us to use the site for camping. Apparently our site was on the edge of an area designated as a protective zone against forest fires, which every summer engulfed many parts of Provence. It meant: no camping, no cooking, no smoking and no wandering around during the night. It was a real blow to us. We had to take our tent to friends in the village for the last few nights before returning to London.

Now we had no other option but to rebuild the ruins of La Bergerie if we wanted to keep the site. The following summer we risked camping on our site by putting up the little tent between ruined walls, absolutely invisible from outside. I started clearing the wilderness around stone walls to make a survey of the building. It was a laborious job of eliminating the entanglement of spiky undergrowth between the rocks, cutting trees and avoiding deep crevasses.

With my survey not accurate to the last centimetre I started to recreate on paper the original sheep barn in order to submit it to Toulon for a building permit. It took some years before we overcame all the ifs and buts of the building department, such as: too small a site (minimum required 5000 sq m.), the signature of a French architect because the R.I.B.A. was not then recognised in France and so on.

The permit finally arrived in the spring of 1984. In summer, still camping in hiding, we began to look for builders, comparing estimates and assessing our resources. My redundancy money was the main basis of the enterprise and construction was to commence in October. I spent a lot of time with the builder, Mr. Albino, discussed the selection of materials and other matters with the Mairie. Mr. Albino was a person of strong character, fearing no obstacle. Looking at a protruding rock in the corner of the ruin he would shrug his shoulders and say "don't worry, I shall deal with it". After settling matters of the Bergerie single handed – because my husband became inactive under the extreme heat of the summer months – I returned to the lake to my favourite corner among the rocks and heather in a little bay. I met Andrew and his companions, who always seem to be there. One day a lady we have been meeting on and off in that spot for years was intrigued by my latest activities. When I mentioned that I would come at the end of October to supervise construction, she asked: "Where you are going to live?", "Under the tent" I answered. After a pause she said: "No, you are not. You are going to stay with me". Did I hear correctly? "Madame, you do not know me, and you don't even know my name, and I do not know yours". "I am called Charlotte and, observing you and your son for the last few years, is the best reference for my offer". She added that the weather in the autumn will be much different and a tent was out of the question – difficult to imagine in the heat of the summer. So, just after All Saints' Day I arrived at Charlotte's villa

Panorama of the Gorge de Verdon

a few kilometres away from the Bergerie and spent two wonderful months there. My "Year in Provence" started and I still do not know when it will finish.

It was the beginning of a great adventure, taking me to a new way of life and to a world of unknown quantities. After an early French breakfast I arrived at the site almost to the minutes with Albino and his team. I was working parallel with them, but much slower, clearing the site as this was not included in the overall estimate, The area designated to contain the "fosse septique" (cesspool) was wildly overgrown and there was a lot of digging, lopping and burning. I joked of being a coloniser working in the jungle.

At midday the workers had a two hours break for lunch, while I stayed on the site till the evening. Our terrain was in the shape of a triangle with a ruin along one side. Its rear wall was the boundary with the neighbouring terrace of olive trees, two meters above our ground. What remained of the original Bergerie was two thirds of the building consisting of one meter high remnants of the end wall. We decided to rebuild a single storey area of about eight by seven meters and to raise a two storey part up to the level of the window sills for future development.

The site of some 1400 sq. m. area of land was sloping down southward and it was quite impenetrable in some parts. Albino had set up the site two weeks before my arrival and I was impressed by the progress. It seemed an imposing project, with the enormous crane in front. I noticed certain discrepancies between the approved drawings and his work. The floor slab was definitely higher than on the drawings and when I questioned this he explained that it was due to the hard rock in the corner. It was not possible to flatten it without the use of dynamite which in turn would have reduced the rest of the ruin to rubble. The only solution was to raise the floor, a solution with which the Council would agree, judging from his experience.

Another disputed matter concerned the concrete block wall that he agreed with my husband to erect in front of the original stone retaining wall, with a void in between for drainage and ventilation. My wish was to have at least part of that beautiful

Andrew at work

stone wall exposed but at the time of my arrival the new block wall of two meters high was already built. When I asked shyly for a few openings, such as windows to be cut in this structure Albino looked at me, than at the wall, scratched his head and declared that he was ready to pull it down and use it for the cesspool at no extra cost, assuring me that with the old stone wall we would have no trouble with damp which turned out not to be the case.

The demolition of the concrete block wall was carried out immediately, leaving only about a half meter high plinth–like wall at floor level with a gutter behind. Both of us were standing in front of an eight meters long stretch of magnificent ancient masonry, contemplating the different shades of pink, cream, white and grey. At times we had bitter arguments about details and I had difficulty in coping with his ignorance of British building standards. For him a damp proof course was not necessary for a stone wall rising from rock foundations, neither a ventilated lobby in front of a bathroom. I had to give in quite often. But Albino was very strong and quick and his team was efficient. Soon he was placing a mono pitch roof over the extended stone walls. It was fascinating to watch the resurrection of a distant past as we tried to keep as much as possible to the original character.

A major innovation was the terrace along the front of the building because of the raised floor inside. It was not included in the drawings nor in the estimate. So I decided to build it myself, leaving only the final paving to Albino. More than ten meters long and a meter and half tall wall to the terrace needed a lot of stones. I gathered them on our site, from the neighbouring woods and builders leftovers by carting them with wheelbarrows. For heavy boulders I used the ancient lever method, rolling the block of stone on the fulcrum with wooden poles. Raising the stones on an ever higher level as the wall grew was an even greater problem and required a lot of acrobatics and perseverance. One of my neighbours came with a plumb line, joking about my hazardous construction, but he did not discourage me. When I uncovered an adjoining ancient garden wall which beautifully matched the one I just had built, I felt complete satisfaction.

A strong dispute arose when we reached roof level. Albino made the eaves of three tiles courses, but I had read that rural buildings should feature only two. "Why are you making a castello out of the Bergerie, Albino?" He laughed and said "your terrace in front the Bergerie entitles it to an upgrade". Then arose the problem of safety. Some of us wanted a balustrade on the terrace but I accepted his suggestion of a row of big pots made in a local pottery, which I later planted with geraniums. The real battle came on the matter of the rainwater gutter when he categorically refused to fix one. "Never on the Bergerie" he shouted. "The rain falls directly from the roof to the ground, this is the tradition". "But now we have the terrace", I said. His retort was "We will protect it". After lunch break he brought a big drum of silicone and sprayed the terrace paving and the lower part of the stone wall generously. It was spectacular to watch in the heavy rain a curtain of water cascading onto the terrace and soaking the wall, while I attempted to gather as much as possible in numerable vessels and bowls. Years later my Polish cousin while holidaying with us, installed a plastic gutter which blended in colour with the stones. At both ends we placed big barrels since when we have had a good supply of water, much needed in dry summer.

Albino finished working before Christmas and we made an "arrosage" (a launch) of the Bergerie with pastis and bottles of wine in the company of our neighbours, Albino, and a few new friends. At the final inspection I pointed out many unfinished parts in the interior, to which he answered "it is up to plasterer". I had an uneasy feeling this would create another predicament, because all our resources were exhausted. Encouragement came from Pamela the painter who pointed to Albino and said: "look at him, this gorilla, if he can do it, so can you"! We all laughed together and celebrated the festive opening of the Bergerie reborn.

During the two months of building works I had a very interesting time at Charlotte's. She lived alone in a not very attractive but tastefully furnished modern concrete villa. After a day on site spent clearing an area for the cess pool and levelling the embankment for kitchen access – jobs not covered by the builder's estimate – I returned to her house. A quick shower followed by a simple snack in the kitchen and I joined Charlotte, who was usually to be found bent over a Jigsaw puzzle in her living room. We watched the news on TV. Later I listened with my limited knowledge of French to her interesting monologue. For example, she remembered a visit with her father, who was an official of the local water board, to the bishop of Toulouse. During lunch the bishop lamented the drying up of the holy spring in Lourdes, hoping for a miracle.

During the war she was actively involved in secret missions, fell in love, married and established home in a monastic chapter house not far from Paris. Due to the poor health of her husband she sold it and moved to Provence. Of her four children only her son Patrick lived in the neighbouring town and visited her with her grandson. I felt a growing bond with her. She was a fascinating person, a walking encyclopaedia and a great connoisseur of the region. She had many hobbies and was surrounded by books on many subjects. She was also a member of several clubs and I joined her in some of her activities, for instance basket weaving.

Most enjoyable were the long cross country walks. We came by car to an agreed point then walked for several hours through beautiful hilly scenery of trees blazing with autumn colours. Under the evergreen oaks and a brilliant blue sky we glimpsed the snowy Alps in the distance – sublime! The group usually consisted of dozen or more participants, some newcomers like me, interested in acquainting themselves with the locality, others were just walkers. We covered many kilometres of mountain paths, crossed many streams and visited many old roadside chapels and crumbling country chateaux which in the past were simply rectangular two – storey blocks with rounded towers.

Land of Templars

Charlotte was a fast driver who took me on a number of wonderful excursions. We traversed most of the mountains above Nice, driving through magnificent gorges and along gushing rivers with spectacular villages perched high above on the rocks. In those days there were still polite policemen with white gloves directing traffic at a typical village bottle–neck, such as in St. Martin Vesubie. We followed the river Var upstream, passing through the fortified town of Entreveaux wits its castle on the cliff reached by seventeen gates, continued through the red rock formation of the Gorge de Daluis. We climbed the Col Champs and descended to the fortress of Colmar–les–Alps in the Verdon valley.

On the way Charlotte pointed out the names of the snow capped peaks in the distance and related many historical anecdotes. She was keenly interested in esoteric beliefs and religious myths. We went to many forgotten ruined places, abandoned Cistercian Abbeys and Templar's chapels between Frejus and Castellane. Our favourite ruin was Valnasque on a hill opposite Callian. This Roman fortress later became an important centre of the order of the Templars until its abolition by Pope Clement V (1312) under pressure from the French King Philippe le Bel. One had a strange feeling of being watched there in these abandoned streets; church was without a roof but had a fine apse. The town ramparts and the impressive Roman tower were entangled with wild vegetation; oak trees grew out of the rubble.

I read in a book entitled "Zig–Zags travers Provence" of 1937 a page devoted to Valnasque where the author said that some-body would one day resurrect the town with all its historic treas-ures. I tried to make a survey of the site but it proved impossible because of the wilderness. Then the right person to do this had appeared – or at least so I thought, in the area. It was agent 007 Sean Connery. He bought neighbouring Chateau Bush, intending to create a golf course. He should have appreciated the historic cause of Vanasque but I could not interest him in it. He later sold the property having met too much opposition to his project.

In 2003 a German software millionaire built there a double golf course with 36 holes, a five star hotel and luxury villas in the same area but Valnasque keeps waiting.

Charlotte was also a great connoisseur of the fruits of the for-est such as mushrooms, wild raspberries, strawberries and the like. With her knowledge of the area we had our baskets full in no time and because she kept a strict diet, most of these delicacies were mine. On weekends showed a great skill in French cooking, but with my limited interest in food I remember only the little quails with a plum inside, and very tasty fowl cooked in the mid-dle of a cabbage with olives and herbs.

My departure to London was marked by a wonderful meal with oysters and champagne. I left at 6a.m. the next morning of

23rd December, still in darkness and with a huge bunch of budding mimosa and very pleasant memories of the last two months. Driving was a tense experience, the whole of France seemed to be on the roads. With long delays I finally reached Paris and was stuck in the traffic on Champs Elysees. At least I could admire the Christmas illuminations. The trees along the Avenue were gleaming with countless white lights. Around Arc de Triomphe hundreds of cars looked as though stranded, inching their way towards the right turning. With the drivers exchanging polite remarks and seasonal greetings it took me a long time before I turned into Avenue de Vagram, found a parking space and rang the door bell of my cousin's home.

The following day I was back in my own home in time to prepare the traditional evening meal, Wigilia – which concluded with attending Midnight Mass at Westminster Cathedral.

During winter I attended evening classes to improve my French. My husband gave me a free hand with the Provancal project: he was quite satisfied with looking after Doozes. Andrew was leading an independent life as a student of medicine in London. Just before Whit Sunday I returned to the south of France.

On arriving at Charlotte I found her packing her car for a short trip to the Midi. I joined her on the spot, leaving my car unpacked in the garage and we drove west. I did not know this part of France so it was an excellent opportunity to explore the area. The weekend holiday made it difficult to find a hotel but eventually we found a vacancy in an old fashioned hotel in Carpentras. It was a good centre for excursions in all directions and we stopped the car whenever the architecture or scenery attracted us. The village of Bories near Gordes was one such place. In Neolithic times this area of about eight kilometres was marked by miles of stone walls enclosing fields and hundreds of small habitations, built as dry stone constructions in the shape of beehives. The word Bori comes from the Latin boria, meaning a shed for bullocks. In recent years more than twenty buildings have been restored with great care, revealing construction details, water proofing, lighting and various adaptations of the interior to make human habitation practical.

The austere character of the place intrigued me as it is known that it was still inhabited at the second half of the 19th century. Similar structures can be found all over the Mediterranean basin and as distant as Ireland and Scotland.

Even more impressive to me was Vaison la Romaine, not far from the magnificent town of Orange. Here the Romans lived with the Celtic people on the opposite banks of the river Ouvveze, embellishing the town with splendid buildings. Wandering about the site two thousand years later I was engulfed by a sad feeling. All that marble glory was now crumbling, faded, and neglected.

I had very different feeling upon arriving at the Fontaine de Vaucluse, where out of a grotto below a cliff emerges a forceful spring to create the river Sorgue. Its erratic flow from (5 to 150 m^3 per second) gave rise to many mystical stories, including the belief that the water originates in the Arctic and passes underground right across Europe. A few years ago the French explorer Jaques Cousteau dived in with his team and swam upward but had to abandon the project after few hundred meters.

Another marvel of the area is Mount Ventoux rising 1909 m. above the rather flat surroundings. It had been climbed by Petrarch in the 14th century. When we reached the summit we found it to be covered with nearly a meter of snow and a strong cold wind was blowing. After a short stroll we descended slowly south down the slopes amongst the larch trees towards the Luberon. We visited the Cistercian Abbey of Senaque, founded in 1148 and then headed home.

I was anxious to see Bergerie again after several months absence. I had mixed feelings of pleasure and disappointment. It looked nice from outside especially the traditional stone masonry and red tile roof, but inside it was a sad sight. A barrel was standing in the middle of a puddle of water and tall weeds were growing from the rear wall. Last December things looked better in candle light, but now, with the sun pouring in through all openings, the faults and problems were all too evident.

I realised that an enormous amount of work had to be done before the house would receive Staszek's approval. To start with I engaged professional plasterers for the ceiling. Watching their swift work I calculated the amount of materials and time required for the walls. I asked them to give me a trial run over a small wall in the bathroom and when workers left I continued on my own. Now I can laugh about it, but at the time it was frightening. The mixture of dry plaster and water prescribed by Albino did not want to stick to the walls. Then I threw the plaster with greater force onto the wetted wall and it worked better. I gathered the bits of fallen plaster back on the trowel and used it to fill the holes and gaps round window sills and unfinished parts of the walls. It turned into a game, like playing with plasticine. When my rubber gloves disintegrated I continued to work with bare hands. I wanted it to have a textured surface to give it a rustic look, so I used all sort of kitchen utensils and broken glass to achieve it.

Soon after I started plastering my nearest neighbour Leslie came for a visit and looking at the miserable state of the walls– and myself – he said mockingly: "Irena, you will be a laughing stock of the area plastering the house by yourself". I felt blood rushing to my cheeks and answered abruptly: "I cannot stop you laughing, but laugh, Leslie, laugh!" and carried on with my work. It was very hot that June and I was yet not used to the local climate so I worked behind closed shutters, opening them after sun set. When half the surface was done I scraped the floor, removed the barrel, installed an old settee which Liz had kept for me, and moved into the Bergerie. Leslie came again, this time to say good bye before going into hospital for observation. The astonishment on his face was most rewarding. "Have you done all this, it looks professional!". It was hearty praise. I kissed him on both cheeks. I slept with all the windows and doors open to let the air in and to feel the pleasure of being close to the surrounding woods, the stars and the space. Early morning I was woken up by an old Spaniel licking my face. This became a sort of ritual. The dog belonged to the guardian of a newly constructed water reservoir known as "chateau d'eau", from which we were the first ones to receive water.

My next priority was to patch up the existing stone walls which, according to Albino, would disintegrate if left unattended. This required the painstaking gradual application of cement mortar to replace the old chalk, whilst also removing debris, roots and moss. Albino was finishing the septic tank with all the necessary chambers required by local byelaws and the distribution channels winding beyond the tank under half a meter deep layers of stones. Then polythene sheets were spread over drained terrain to contain the water below a final layer of topsoil. Albino declared that the latter item was not included in his work and advised us to engage a gardener, adding that the site should be covered with at least 15 cm. of topsoil. After checking my budget I ordered a lorry load of soil from a local firm, but when unloaded it looked more like builder's rubble than earth. There were lumps of blue clay, broken bricks and china, and a few solitary iris roots. So, most of summer passed wheeling in the precious earth, some of it collected from the places on our site and from the nearby woods. Everyone who could help was welcome.

I had some fun with the final touch by constructing a life size sheep from a skeleton of scrap metal and surplus plaster. Staszek expressed the wish to have a symbol for the Bergerie which would serve as a focal point. He approved my sheep for this purpose.

Then apparently we needed a letter box. The postman urged me to buy one from his catalogue. But I made one with a plastic bucket on string. Then I created my own letter–box – a la Provencale – a rough stone column with an opening under a tiled roof.

IX. LIFE AROUND CALLIAN

In 1985 at the beginning of his medical studies in London Andrew made a date with a colleague who with her mother was preparing a car tour of France. They were to meet one day at 10 a.m. at the entrance to the Foundation Maeght, an art centre near Vence a few kilometres from Nice. This has been decided in London and to Andrew's surprise he had to wait only ten minutes before they arrived. It was a place he had known for years, being charmed by its position in the beautiful park of sculptures and the small chapel with its incredible echo. Singing a school hymn there gave the impression of hearing a big choir. We used to go there to visit exhibitions in the modern gallery and the park and to take pictures beside Giacometti's elongated statues in the courtyard.

Now he was bringing the ladies by a special route via Coussols to the Bergerie before finishing the day with wind surfing on the lake. By September the site looked quite organised and we concentrated on the finishing touches. Great help was the village dumping ground where one could find lots of things from motorist parts to kitchen utensils, garden plants, pieces of furniture and much else. Each visit brought something exciting – yet another chair, a cupboard or a kettle. Wooden boards were very much needed for making steps and a table under an oak tree. Sometimes I came there across elegant ladies, hands in gloves who were sorting the heaps of rubbish to select something special. A few years later the system had changed and one had to make arrangement to deposit rubbish.

Staszek came towards the end of September "for the inspection", and passed everything with great enthusiasm. He studied the electrical conduits, considering installing new wiring himself with the assistance of Antoine, our neighbour, who rewired his house. But in the end we engaged a reputable electrician. One day Charlotte arrived with a magnificent oleander which we planted as a focal point on the terrace. She was moving to Cannes and handed on to us a number of interesting items: an old horse harness, some ceramics, a huge earthenware pot made by her father, a big mirror, kitchen cabinets and a wheel barrow, some tools and an ancient barbecue. I would miss her and hoped she would return.

Staszek struck up a friendship with Albino and before leaving for London asked him to begin building the second stage of the house when he had the time. With his usual charming grin he said: "I will pay you when I can". They laughed and Albino nodded.

To my surprise noise and clatter woke me up next Monday morning. It was Albino with his big crane, his team of workers and a lorry full of sand and cement. They started work immediately by erecting a scaffold along the walls and after clearing the ground inside, poured concrete for the floor. I created the base of a large fireplace in the corner of the main room, extending it at one side to make a sizeable bench. After lining it with fireproof bricks and forming a smoke shelf along the back wall I had a lot of trouble constructing the hood though it looked simple in the drawing. I had to ask Albino for help.

It was not a conventional fireplace, it was one with a big arch in the front and a smaller one on the side. Originally it was not considered necessary for our summer visits, but when it became obvious we would be there may be over Christmas it became essential. Albino was at first apprehensive about its shape and our plan to smoke sausages in the chimney but in the end he was so pleased with it he insisted on plastering it himself. (see p. 167)

The next day was the official opening of the fireplace with the usual "arrosage" ritual. We invited the nearest neighbours, our friends and their friends. From Julia and David we received an enormous log decorated with red ribbons, and from the others lots of bottles for the "christening". Unfortunately, Liz was alone by now because Leslie died few months earlier. We were surrounded by lot of interesting people but not very many locals.

Some Provenceaux were quite hostile to foreigners. Our neighbour, with his neglected olive grove directly behind the Bergerie once outpoured his bitterness to me: "I am a local man and I was refused a building permit for rebuilding the ruins on my site. But permits were quickly given to strangers". He was wielding his fists about to strike. I encouraged him to fight for his rights. Gradually we became friends, and he once arrived with a bucket of fish which he caught in the lake. "For the bergère", he said graciously. At last I was accepted as one of the locals.

Newcomers to the area hailed from the whole of Europe. Some spent their holidays in their villas and then shut them up for the winter, while others settled there for good. Some formed active group and I joined Liz in her Scandinavian meetings.

Both of us took part in a special event: The historic Rally of Cannes. Liz agreed to be the driver and I was to prepare answers to hundreds of questions. I spent several sleepless nights pouring over books from the public library – formerly the Rothschild's villa in Cannes. An hour later my car had been broken into and my overnight bag had gone missing. With some difficulty I found the police station and reported the theft listing the missing items. When the officer on duty failed to include on his list my nightdress I objected. He raised his eyes and said with a smile: "A nightdress? They do not exist on the Cote d' Azur". Well I thought, each country has its peculiarities and henceforth decided to go native in the heat of the August nights. I began to implement the policeman's motto at Bergerie and lakeside for an early morning swim, especially after I witnessed a middle aged woman drop her gown on the shore of the lake and step into the water like Botticeli's Primavera. This was the rare treat as the priority was the Bergerie, where the walls were rising fast.

Going back to the rally – it was the first inter – European event which started with glamour at the Palace de Festivals at midday and had a spectacular finale in the evening. The number of participants was truly impressive and I doubted our chances of success, looking at so many confident faces. Finding the ten places from the description was easy, but to answer the questionnaires collected at each check point was more difficult as most of them had nothing in common with the material I studied for two weeks or more. Before handing over the papers we sat on the kerbside, glass of Vermouth in hand, digesting the questions. I still remember two I could not answer. First, what was the price of land in Cannes in 1836? Second, what was the name of the prisoner on the island of St. Marguerite who, after serving his sentence of twenty years did not want to leave prison? We had to hand in our papers at a certain time at the Palais de Festivals and after a lengthy wait we heard the results.

We won first prize for foreigners, having the largest number of correct answers. Only one Frenchman answered the second question. The prize was a bottle of champagne which pleased Liz, and a huge cup, like a Russian samovar, which I took back to London with me. Soon after this Liz was visited by her stepson Henrick from Denmark. He wanted to see the place where his father died. Liz was looking for some attractions for Henrick, who unfortunately suffered from schizophrenia and she brought him over while Andrew was on a short visit. Henrick saw me painting the kitchen wall with white emulsion round a sketch of a palm tree. He looked at it and said: "I can paint too". "Well, you have the rest of the wall at your disposal" I said. He smiled and then went home.

He returned a few hours later with an attractive sketch done with great accomplishment and enlarged it onto the wall in black chalk. He created a mural of about ten metres square, representing an enormous bird with spread wings and formidable claws hovering over a delicate palm tree. Henrick's mural became a permanent feature and evoked considerable comment. Luckily, he did not have time to colour it so it blended very well with the interior and is not overpowering.

Albino roofed over the second part of the house and instructed me in preparations for tiling the floor. Three cubic meters of gravel had to be brought inside and spread and spread over the concrete to the thickness of five centimetres, covering the service conduits in both parts of the house. Bringing buckets and buckets of gravel was a tedious job, but later it gave a pleasant feeling of camping on the beach. Some time later I covered it with heavy duty polythene sheeting as a damp proof course, over which Albino laid polysterene slabs as insulation and a special screed to receive the "terre quite" tiles. These were soaking for two weeks in a barrel of water. We selected big square tiles of a mellow honey colour, which harmonised with the old stones of the rear wall.

Keeping warm by the fireplace at Bergerie

The weather was deteriorating and we had to borrow an electric heater to accelerate the drying. It was a great day when the power was switched on. The first moment of dazzling light made us almost sorry for the abandoned candles. We were soon reconciled to the change. The electrician even managed to fit a lighting point in the middle of Henrick's mural without destroying a single line of it. Staszek arrived during the final stage of floor tiling and we kept out of the way of builders. Knowing my love of swimming he encouraged me to swim across the lake, even though it was early November. Nobody was around, only Staszek. He was waiting on the shore in a sheepskin coat, with another one ready for me.

One night soon we were confronted with a real nightmare. A thunderstorm with vivid flashes of lightening gave the impression that sky was falling on us. We got up to find ourselves ankle deep in water. At daybreak I ran to Liz to call Albino from her phone. He calmed me down, assuring me that our case was nothing compared to others, who were literally washed out of their beds. His own priority was to unblock the road between the villages. At that moment Liz called me to watch the news on television. I recognised our beautiful village shown on the screen as one of the powerful storms which swept over the south of France during the night. The amount of devastation was horrendous. Entire roads were swept away, big rocks landed on the roofs of houses, trees were uprooted, town squares covered with sand and gravel. By Bergerie a stream was roaring down obliterating the lane.

The house, being at the bottom of a terraced mountain, received huge quantities of water that flooded us out. But soon the hot sun dried the ground in front and we could wash the muddy carpets and blankets, drying them on a line between trees. It took several days to dry them. It was not the end of capricious weather. At the beginning of December white ground frost covered the area and the water in the barrels full of the remaining floor tiles had a layer of solid ice on top. Lower down on the plain below Callian the temperature dropped to - 8°C. In these harsh conditions we started our journey back. All along our favourite Route de Soleil the countryside offered a stern wintry scene and only when we reached Aix–en–Provence did it begin to mellow and get warmer. We arrived in London to warm weather.

My third season in Bergerie was glorious. Immediately on arrival I had a sensation in tune with Lord Brougham's inscription over the door of his villa "Eleonora" in Cannes: "INVENI PORTUM" (Enter the door). The finishing touches to the stone walls were like child's play compared with the treatment of the floor tiles. On Albino's instructions, I applied fifteen coats of a special mixture of turpentine and linseed oil, rubbing each tile with a cloth till no more could be absorbed. After a pause of two weeks the floor had to be washed with a sealant which imparted a slight shine. The effect was excellent and everyone liked it.

Finally we arrived at the stage of arranging furniture in the second part of the house, beginning with an oak table Albino had rescued from a demolition site. I paid Liz for some bedroom furniture she gathered from her friends and from the nearby supermarket came half a dozen plastic chairs for the terrace. Two neighbours, Mado and Pierre, gave us two old beds and some cutlery.

Now the Bergerie was finally suitable for human habitation – if slightly gipsy in character. Cooking was still done by a camping stove. But this suited me fine – I had no ambition to transform a "cattle shed into a Mediterranean villa". The site was still a bit wild, but the triangle over the septic tank was already covered by masses of poppies, herbs and pretty flowering weeds.

On the terrace there were pots of geraniums and petunias and at the corner by the steps was a clump of pampas grass brought by Andrew from the nearby woods. Wild thyme flourished all over the site and looked beautiful at flowering time. There were also wild lavender, sarriette, marjoram and rosemary. The site was green and full of colour until mid – June, turning gradually yellow to brown, finally becoming like a continuation of the rocks, merging into a stony soul of Provence. I simply loved it all. To provide some shade for the terrace during hot summer days Andrew brought from London his enormous Chinese umbrella, but it was blown away in the wind together with its bamboo stand. So I decided

Interior of Bergerie

to build a large concrete table under the oak trees, not too far from the kitchen.

The construction entailed a lot of difficulties. Two massive legs were formed with plastic pots which Liz brought from Denmark. The two meter long slab had to be formed by shuttering, using reinforcement rods and mesh inserted before I could start pouring in the concrete. The concrete was carried in buckets from the bottom of the slope. The whole operation took several days but the table was eventually finished. It was a pleasant sight and floor placed on top seemed to be perfectly level.

The following morning I discovered to my horror that some parts of the table had sunk and several tiles in the middle were out of plumb. At first I was very disappointed but time softened the blow. It has served us well ever since. Behind the table I cut into a rocky slope to form a bench with enough room to seat half a dozen people. We stretched a hammock between a tall pine and a rugged oak tree, where I still like to pass a hot afternoon reading, planning the next task or just falling asleep.

As the years passed I suffered some bereavement in my family. My parents and one of my brothers died in the seventies, and in August 1990 my husband died of cancer after a year-long brave fight. It is impossible to convey the depth of my personal feelings. I can find no words eloquent enough to express the enormity of my loss. Perhaps the funeral speech of Jurek, son of a very close family friend manages to convey at least some part of my husband's wonderful personality. (See "Farewell Staszek").

I was unable to visit Bergerie for over a year. When I did return there a nice surprise was awaiting me in the flourishing cypress tree planted by Staszek two years earlier. It had fractured during his illness at the spot where it was tied to its support. Now it was reaching upward again with its healthy little branches wrapped tightly around the stem.

The Bergerie

Charlotte moved back to the country but unfortunately with much reduced mobility following a stroke. Liz decided to leave for faraway Australia to join her family. I took an instant liking to the new owners, Lora and Friderick, who fell in love with their house and were spending most of the year there. In 1998 Andrew married lovely Lucinda, his wonderful companion. They visited Provence on their way from honeymoon in Switzerland to stop for a week in Callian. I prepared a welcoming surprise for them in the Bergerie – a new bathroom in the second part of the house, known as Andrew's wing. It was installed by young Vincent, as our dear Albino, only two years after Staszek's death had also died of cancer. For the newlyweds I prepared a splendid reception, almost a second wedding. It was a grand garden party with food, drinks and toasts to the newlyweds including a poem written for the occasion by Friderick.

Andrew was not yet fully recovered from an accident sustained before the wedding. They stopped for lunch with some friends on the way to another friend's wedding and Andrew, always high spirited, joined children on a rope swing which hung from a tree in the garden. Suddenly the rope broke, and Andrew crashed down. Lucinda was panic – stricken to see her future husband's green complexion and motionless on the ground. Fortunately, their wedding could go ahead – Andrew fortified by several injections – so no one noticed that he had four broken ribs and a perforated lung.

The wedding went ahead but the planned honeymoon to the Galapagos Island and Peru had to be called off. Instead they took a quiet convalescence in an Alpine chalet.

Soon after Andrew and Lucinda left Bergerie we suffered another deluge caused by heavy rain. A flood of water gushed through the stone wall next to the fireplace and poured over the channel onto the floor. I emptied bucket after bucket of water until the rain slowed down in the evening. After mopping the floor with towels I fell asleep exhausted.

I was woken up in the morning by a loud knocking. A neighbour, Pierre, walked in determined to take action against the floods. He brought a sketch indicating all stages which needed to be carried through and the telephone number of a builder with a mechanical digger. The digger arrived the same afternoon and the excavation behind the wall was on the way. An excavation two metres wide and more than two metres deep was created along the wall. Pierre, a mining engineer by profession, was determined to find the source of the water. When the digger stopped against a solid block of rock he knew he had found it. About half way along the fifteen metres wall of the building this rock was touching the stone wall about half a metre above floor level and channelling water into the interior. It took almost two days for workmen to flatten the rock. Under Pierre's instructions we set out to construct a drainage system. For reasons of cost the waterproof rendering, considered best for the job, was replaced by extra heavy duty plastic used for lining swimming pools.

Fixing the three metres wide rolls was very difficult. Pierre brought with him two strong men, guests of the family who arrived to help in harvesting olives: their help was essential in the case of Bergerie. Luckily, the weather held out but the evening sun set early so we had to work by torch light. We were the living proof of Pierre's saying: "A good neighbour is not there just to exchange sweet words across the fence, but who is there when you need him".

Then we placed precast concrete channels at the bottom of the trench and then covered them with protective sheeting and a layer of stones. Finally, digger shovelled back the earth. Pierre worked like Hercules, shifting huge stones. I called him Superman! A week later we celebrated the completion of this heroic work with champagne at Pierre and Elisabeth's house.

The rear drainage had been on our minds ever since first acquiring the Bergerie, but since it was at the boundary of the site we needed permission of the neighbours. This turned out to be difficult. All changed for the better later on when we bought the land behind the Bergerie, consisting of nine terraces of old olive trees. I had no ambition to become a producer of olive oil anyway, but since it was obligatory to cleat an area of fifty metres round a house as precaution against the fires which rage in Provence almost every summer, we had no option but to clear and maintain the terraces. With an electric cutter presented by our visitors Magda and Zygmunt, it was easy to clear the wilderness. There were pleasant surprises which exposed the wonderful forms of the gnarled old tree trunks, dramatically shaped protruding roots and twisted branches.

Equally beautiful were the walls supporting the terraces, true marvels of dry stone masonry which incorporated the existing rock formation. Unfortunately some of them are beginning to crumble. Unveiling the terraces gave me enormous pleasure. I began to name rocks according to their shapes. There was Fortresse, Arc of Alliance, Wailing Wall, Rock of Zion and at the top my favourite: The bridge of the Argonaut's captain from where the breathtaking view was overwhelming.

One day along came Fernand, the local celebrity for cultivation of olives. He gave me strict instructions what to do with the neglected grove. "You must dig a metre wide ring around each tree, half metre deep minimum and remove all parasitic roots before applying some fertilizer". By now I was feeling like a real colonist, with a shovel in my hands and a mighty backache. The wild untidy hill changed miraculously into an area animated by the sculptural forms of olive trees.

Andrew energetically cleared the woods to within fifty metres on the other side of the road, but anything beyond he would not touch.

The top terrace concealed another mystery. When clearing around a small stone ruin there I came across a big rock in the corner with an arch at the bottom. There my broomstick found the crack in the rock floor. I stood bewildered, wandered what else I had uncovered. I called Pierre who came with mining equipment and we decided to explore further.

Before that absorbing activity we enjoyed an exciting evening on 24 of June, St. John's day. Inspired by the beauty of the view from the terrace towards the "Massif de L'Esterel" and a glimpse of the sea between the mountains and charmed by sweet scent of the herbs and the full moon that night we organised with our neighbours Lora and Friderick a Fool Moon Picnic in the most elevated point of the olive grove. Several friends joined us, bringing special delicacies of various parts of Europe. Drinking and eating, we waited for the moon to rise. To enhance the view we decided to cut down two pine trees which were obscuring the Moon. In so doing we also strengthened a few of the nearest olive trees as they cannot thrive with pines near them. Then in the magic lunar light we recited poems in six different languages. It was quite stimulating and very friendly.

The next few days I spent digging and scraping in a slowly revealed cave. Pierre threw himself into this operation and we were brimming with enthusiasm and expectations. Shall we make some spectacular find? Alas, nothing of the kind, but it was fun just the same.

Pierre digging in the cave

During my sejours in Provence I lived through many wonderful moments, visited magic places and met many charming people. Once, swimming in the large pool of our friends, I heard the tune of violin playing a sublime piece of Mendelssohn. I tried to make myself invisible and motionless as I watched a young man under an arch where he was producing his heavenly music. Than a face with enormous eyes and a long hair tied in a pony tail appeared over the edge of the pool and he introduced himself as Olivier. With a lump in my throat I said that his music was too great to be played to such a small audience, to which he replied: "Well, after tomorrow I shall be playing in the cathedral at Grasse". I shall be there, I said. Lora and Frederick who loved music, agreed to join me but with some slight apprehension because the concert had not been advertised locally; little we realise that Olivier was one of the top French violinists. After the concert Friderick kissed my hand.

Among the people I came to love is Lucienne, a native Provencalle and a person of great humanity, gentleness, good humour and common sense. She lives alone in a house behind the chapel of Notre Dame de la Rose by the bamboo – lined little river Camiolle and its wide basin, where Staszek loved watching the movements of two enormous carp. She has fruit trees, rows of raspberry bushes and lots of vegetables which she is pleased to share with friends and neighbours, us amongst them.

After each visit we go home with a car boot full of lovely produce of the land. This might include the occasional bottle of olive oil, with the injunction to Andrew written on the label. "Never in the frying pan, dear doctor, never!" She told us a great deal about olive grove cultivation, holding up the bottle of golden liquid to the light.

For twenty years she helped her brother Fernand cultivating the trees, climbing up from the village almost four kilometres every day, pruning, moving and watering until the harvest.

Picking the olives was done by hand with a basket, while the ones dropping on the ground were collected on a close net spread around each tree. There were several hundred trees in Fernand's grove, so the harvest extended sometimes from Christmas till Easter. The collected olives were taken to the village olive mill for pressing. It requires on average five kilograms of olives for one litre of oil! No wonder Lucienne had such a great respect for the precious liquid. Every time we drive through fields of olive trees stretching for miles along the roads, I see not only their beauty, but also sense the hard work and loving that has nurtured them through centuries.

Lucienne and Andrew

Finally, I must mention the cause of the Mystery of the Templars, which Charlotte had read about. We were determined to solve it and to find the hiding place of their supposed treasure. The book gave a quite detailed description of the location, referring to "Little Brittany" in the neighbourhood of the Gorges de

Verdon. Charlotte suffered a stroke but she could drive her specially adapted car and walk a little with a stick. We began the search covering quite a large area, but with no luck. One autumn Sunday we invited Victoria, an ex–president of the Walking Club, to join us. She knew the most secret paths, but the afternoon again passed without success. Disappointed and cold we stopped at a roadside café. While my companions visited the next door flour mill I stood at the entrance looking inside, when a miller in his white cap appeared: "What I can do for you, Madam?", he said. Thoughtfully I answered: "You? Nothing Monsieur, I am looking for the spirit of King Arthur and his knights" at which his face lit up. "You are familiar with the story?" he exclaimed, pulling me to the corner of the café, hiding me from the other people.

After some discussion about the book, the castle and the chapel, the Templars and their treasures, he agreed to show me and my friends the way to the secret place of King Arthur and the treasure included, on condition that we make the last hundred metres on foot. In first gear Charlotte drove us across rocks, upturned roots, streams and dense forest until we reached a grass covered hill bang in the middle of the mountains of Verdon. There were no ruins in sight and in the setting sun the emptiness of the area had a spooky atmosphere. The mountain peaks facing the setting sun revealed a play of colours from white to gold to blazing crimson, while the lower slopes were turning to violet and black. Charlotte stopped the car and gave me fifteen minutes to explore the top. Victoria, not much drawn to mysteries, decided to walk back to the main road and look for mushrooms on the way. Almost running, I reached a big open plateau with a few old trees and a crumbling chateau three storeys high with circular corner towers. A barking dog ran towards me and the heavy door opened and a tall man with silver hair appeared. This had to be Monsieur Andre, the guardian of the castle, the writer and philosopher described by the miller.

I ran towards him and spontaneously threw myself at his neck with the joy of having arrived at the end of a long search. This surreal, solitary figure of ascetic appearance in a long coat, bearded face and most of his teeth missing, the inevitable walking stick – who was he? To me he could have been the embodiment of any of the legendary heroes: King Arthur, the Knight of the Round Table, Don Quichote, the Templar, or Veris, the hero of Andre's strange book. Perhaps one day I shall find out more.

Canyon du Verdon

X. ANDREW AND THE POPE JOHN PAUL II

During his visit to the United Kingdom in 1982, John Paul celebrated mass for the Polish Community at the Crystal Palace Sports Centre in London. Early on Sunday morning the stadium was packed with thousands of people, some of whom travelled overnight from distant parts of the country. The grounds were like a park with vast lawns and flower beds, the delicate spring foliage was emerging on the trees. Through it ran a long path connecting landing platform for helicopter, with policemen on both sides. On the approach of the "Pope–Mobil" the congregation stood up clapping their hands, a little too lethargically for my liking. When the Pontif rejoined his vehicle after the mass, they clapped again. The Pope standing in his vehicle circled the track, blessing the crowd. When the car was nearing the exit close to our grandstand, Andrew suddenly threw himself backwards and with an "excuse me" jumped over several rows of seats to get to the top, finally disappearing behind the parapet wall of the stadium. Greatly alarmed standing on top of embankment, I had a striking view. The Pope–Mobil was travelling along the lane edged by policemen, and in the distance I saw Andrew returning towards the stadium. In his white cricket outfit he looked like a magnificent big bird flying with outstretched arms. Climbing back onto the bank he asked "Did you see me? I had a sudden urge to pass my personal message to the Pope because I heard so many fascinating stories about him during my skiing holidays in the Tatra mountains". Kardinal Wojtyla, as he was then, was a very popular figure among the gorals. And besides, he was a good skier! So, Andrew continued, "I quickly ran down the slope, in time to meet the Pope's vehicle emerging from the gate, and followed it running a few metres behind. Then I put my hands to my mouth and shouted in highlander's dialect:

"Hej, Gazdo, syckiego Wam najlepsego z calego serca zycem"
– (Hey, Great Farmer, I wish you all the best from the bottom of my heart).

The Pope's reaction was marvellous. He smiled broadly and carried on talking. Unfortunately I couldn't hear very well, but I felt the connection which ended with his big sign of Cross. I shall remember this for the rest of my life".

XI. FAREWELL STASZEK

We have helped our friend Staszek Sikorski to start his last journey. I hope that we will be as kind to his memory as the earth is to his remains. I hope this for two reasons.

Primarily, because in our culture, we believe there should be nothing but good spoken of the dead. It is unjust to pour more bitterness into the cup that was the earthly portion of the departed. Staszek had bitterness enough to swallow. A lesser man would have become introverted and vengeful. But Staszek was not a lesser man. He was open, warm, and generous.

And in addition, because we will no longer hear his unique voice in our discussions. No matter how much some of us differed from his opinions, he always made his point clearly, and defended himself most articulately. Let us not take advantage of his silence to have the last word.

I believe that Staszek's uniqueness lay in three aspects of his person.

- Firstly, he was witty without being trivial. Endowed with an exceptionally keen intelligence, he spoke with authority.

- Secondly, he did not allow himself to be crushed by the burden of his wartime experiences nor by our general Polish history. He lived his life as would any normal man of superior wit. That is, he looked for and found a way of life that suited him and his nearest. He used the power of his reason to accept or reject convention. In his personal life he embodied perfectly the existentialist principle that man is free.

- Thirdly, he was confident enough within himself to ask radical questions. Not to question is born of fear and timidity. He enjoyed a vigorous dialectic firmly rooted in humanism.

I will never be able to see Staszek through the eyes of his contemporaries. For some, I know, he touched raw nerves and questioned what they considered should be beyond dispute. His arguments were controversial, and not everybody understood them. To us, the younger generation, he towered head and shoulders above the rest. He was the living proof that we could be everything we wanted to be and still be Polish. I cherish his memory and mourn him not so much as a friend (I didn't know him well enough for that) but as one of the heroes of my youth.

Jerzy Kirakowski London 3rd September, 1990.

EPILOGUE

The following years were shaped by pattern of time spent, almost regularly, between England, France and Poland punctuated by an occasional trip to more distant parts of the globe.

Andrew with his family in England moved me towards a closer attachment to my adopted country, where I had my first taste of freedom and where I enjoyed the most productive years of my life. I enjoy revisiting many anthropological sites, bound up with the development of human existence throughout the centuries in this country. In the same spirit we liked to visit Maiden Castle, The Pyramid known as Silbury Hill, Hadrian's Wall and many other hallowed sites. But I also loved Doozes, which had such a strong emotional hold on Staszek.

Poland has an almost magic power over me, Poland is my childhood and my family. Polish is my mother tongue. I love the beauty of its countryside which is imbedded deep in my psyche, – The Bialowieza Forest, the majestic Giewont in the Tatra mountains, the marvels of Wieliczka, they are all present in my mental and spiritual make–up.

But Provence is my earthly PARADISE. I feel my roots there now, in the rocky ground. Surrounded by so much of beauty, the azure sky, the pure air saturated with the aroma of wild flowers and herbs, the wide horizon dotted with small villages perched on top of mountains, and rocks vibrating the eternal metamorphosis of life and death. Here is the kind of sustenance I need to carry on a meaningful existence.

"Witch of l'Esterel"

1. POLAND IN THE SECOND WORLD WAR

The invasion of Poland in 1939

On September 1 1939, 1.8 million German troops invaded Poland on three fronts; East Prussia in the north, Germany in the west and Slovakia in the south. They had 2600 tanks against the Polish 180, and over 2000 aircraft against the Polish 420. Their „Blitzkrieg" tactics, coupled with their bombing of defenceless towns and refugees, had never been seen before and, at first, caught the Poles off–guard. By September 14th. Warsaw was surrounded. At this stage the Poles reacted, holding off the Germans at Kutno and regrouping behind the Wisla (Vistula) and Bzura rivers. Although Britain and France declared war on September 3rd the Poles received no help – yet it had been agreed that the Poles should fight a defensive campaign for only 2 weeks during which time the Allies could get their forces together and attack from the west. There are many "myths" that surround the September Campaign; the fictional Polish cavalry charges against German tanks (actually reported by the Italian press and used as propaganda by the Germans), the alleged destruction of the Polish Air Force on the ground, or claims that Polish armour failed to achieve any success against the invaders. In reality, and despite the fact that Poland was only just beginning to modernise her armed forces and had been forced (by Britain and France) to delay mobilisation (which they claimed might be interpreted as aggressive behaviour) so that, at the time of invasion, only about one–third of her total potential manpower was mobilised, Polish forces ensured that the September campaign was no „walk–over". The Wehrmacht had so under–rated Polish anti–tank capabilities (the Polish– designed anti–tank gun was one of the best in the world at that time) that they had gone into action with white „balkankreuz", or crosses, prominently displayed in eight locations; these crosses made excellent aiming points for Polish gun –sights and forced the Germans to radically rethink their national insignia, initially overpainting them in yellow and then, for their

193

later campaigns, adopting the modified „balkankreuz" similar to that used by the Luftwaffe. The recently–designed 7TP „czolg lekki", or light tank, the first in the world to be designed with a diesel engine, proved to be superior to German tanks of the same class (the PzKpfw I and II) inflicting serious damage to the German forces, limited only by the fact that they were not used in concentrated groups. They were absorbed by the Germans into their own Panzer divisions at the end of the campaign.

On September 17th Soviet forces invaded from the east. Warsaw surrendered 2 weeks later, the garrison on the Hel peninsula surrendered on October 2nd, and the Polesie Defence group, after fighting on two fronts against both German and Soviet forces, surrendered on October 5th. The Poles had held on for twice as long as had been expected and had done more damage to the Germans than the combined British and French forces were to do in 1940. The Germans lost 50,000 men, 697 planes and 993 tanks and armoured cars.

Thousands of soldiers and civilians managed to escape to France and Britain whilst many more went „underground". A government–in–exile was formed with Wladyslaw Raczkiewicz as President and General Wladyslaw Sikorski as Prime Minister.

The Fourth Partition

Under the German–Soviet pact Poland was divided; the Soviets took, and absorbed into the Soviet Union, the eastern half (Byelorussia and the West Ukraine), the Germans incorporated Pomerania, Posnania and Silesia into the Reich whilst the rest was designated as the General–Gouvernement (a colony ruled from Krakow by Hitler's friend, Hans Frank).

In the Soviet zone 1.5 million Poles (including women and children) were transported into labour camps in Siberia and other areas. Many thousands of captured Polish officers were shot at several secret forest sites; the first to be discovered being Katyn, near Smolensk. The Germans declared their intention of eliminating the Polish race (a task to be completed by 1975) alongside the Jews. This process of elimination, the „Holocaust", was carried out systematically. All members of the „intelligentsia" were hunted down in order to destroy Polish culture and leadership (many were originally – „terminated at Oswiecim – better known by its German name, Auschwitz).

Secret universities and schools, a „Cultural Underground", were formed (the penalty for belonging to one was death). In the General–Gouvernement there were about 100,000 secondary school pupils and over 10,000 university students involved in secret education.

The Polish–Jews were herded into Ghetto's where they were slowly starved and cruelly offered hopes of survival but, in fact, ended up being shot or gassed, In the end they were transported, alongside non–Jewish Poles, Gypsies and Soviet POWs, to extermiation camps such as Auschwitz and Treblinka; at Auschwitz over 4 million were exterminated 2000 concentration camps were built in Poland, which became the major site of the extermination programme, since this was where most of the intended victims lived.

Many non–Jawish Poles were either transported to Germany and used as slave labour or simply executed in the cities. The Germans would round–up and kill indiscriminately as a punishment for any underground or anti–German or pro–Jewish activity. In the countryside they kept prominent citizens as hostages who would be executed if necessary. Sometimes they liquidated whole villages; at least 300 villages were destroyed. Hans Frank said, „If I wanted to put up a poster for every seven Poles shot, the forests of Poland would not suffice to produce the paper for such posters".

Despite such horror the Poles refused to give in or cooperate (there were no Polish collaborators as in other occupied countries). The Polish Underground or AK (Armia Krajowa or Home

Army) was the largest in Europe with 400,000 men. The Jewish resistance movement was set up separately because of the problem of being imprisoned within the ghettos. Both these organisations caused great damage to the Nazi military machine. Many non–Jewish Poles saved the lives of thousands of Jews despite the fact that the penalty, if caught, was death (in fact, Poland was the only occupied nation where aiding Jews was punishable by death).

The Poles fight on all fronts with the allies

The Polish Army, Navy and Air Force reorganised abroad and continued to fight the Germans. In fact they have the distinction of being the only nation to fight on every front in the War. In 1940 they fought in France, in the Norwegian campaign they earned a reputation for bravery at Narvik, and in Africa the Carpathian Brigade fought at Tobruk.

Polish Squadrons played an important role in the Battle of Britain, accounting for 12% of all German aircraft destroyed at the cost of 33 lives. By the end of the war they had flown a total of 86,527 sorties, lost 1669 men and shot down 500 German planes and 190 V1 rockets.

The Polish Navy, which had escaped intact, consisted of 60 vessels, including 2 cruisers, 9 destroyers and 5 submarines (one of which was the famous „Orzel") which were involved in 665 actions at sea. The first German ship sunk in the war was sunk by Polish ships. The Navy also took part in the D–Day landings.

When the Soviet Union was attacked by Germany, in June 1941, Polish POWs were released from prison camps and set up an army headed by General Anders. Many civilians were taken under the protection of this army which was allowed to make its way to Persia (modern–day Iran) and then on to Egypt. This army, the Polish Second Corps, fought with distinction in Italy, their most notable victory being that at Monte Cassino, in May 1944, and which opened up the road to Rome for the Allies as a whole. One of the „heroes" of the Polish Second Corps was Wojtek, a brown bear adopted in Iran as their mascot; at Monte Cassino Wojtek actually helped in the fighting by carrying ammunition for the guns. He died, famous and well–loved, in Edinburgh Zoo in 1964, aged 22.

All the Polish forces took part in the Allied invasion of Europe and liberation of France, playing a particularly crucial role in the significant Battle of the Falaise Gap. The Polish Parachute Brigade took part in the disastrous Battle of Arnhem in Holland. In 1945, the Poles captured the German port of Wilhelmshaven.

In 1943 a division of Polish soldiers was formed in Russia under Soviet control and fought on the Eastern Front. They fought loyally alongside the Soviet troops, despite the suffering they had experienced in Soviet hands, and they distinguished themselves in breaking through the last German lines of defence, the „Pomeranian Rampart", in the fighting in Saxony and in the capture of Berlin.

The „Home Army", under the command of General Stefan Rowecki (code–named „Grot"), and after his capture in 1943 (he was later murdered), by General Tadeusz Komorowski (code –named „Bor"), fought a very varied war; at times in open combat in brigade or division strength, at times involved in sabotage, often acting as execution squads eliminating German officials, and often fighting a psychological campaign against German military and civilians. It was a costly war since the Germans always took reprisals.

The Intelligence Service of the Home Army captured and sent parts of the V1 to London for examination, providing information on German military movements (giving advanced warning of the German plan to invade Russia), and gave the RAF full information about Peenemunde, where the Germans were producing V2 rockets.

Betrayal of the Poles by the allies

The crime of Katyn was discovered in 1943 and created a rift in Polish–Soviet relations. From now on the Home Army was attacked by Soviet propaganda as collaborating with the Germans and being called on to rise against the Germans once the Red Army reached the outskirts of Warsaw.

Secretly, at Teheran, the British and Americans agreed to letting the Russians profit from their invasion of Poland in 1939 and allowing them to keep the lands that had been absorbed. The „accidental" death of General Sikorski at this time helped keep protests at a minimum.

When the Russians crossed into Poland the Home Army co-operated in the fight against the Germans and contributed greatly to the victories at Lwow, Wilno and Lublin only to find themselves surrounded and disarmed by their „comrades–in –arms" and deported to labour camps in Siberia.

On August 1, 1944, with the Russian forces on the right bank of the Vistula, the Home Army rose in Warsaw; the Warsaw Rising. Heroic street–fighting involving the whole population, using the sewers as lines of communication and escape, under heavy bombardment, lasted for 63 days. The city was completely destroyed. Not only did the Russians cease to advance but they also refused to allow Allied planes to land on Russian airfields after dropping supplies. After surrendering many civilians and soldiers were executed or sent to concentration camps to be exterminated and Warsaw was razed to the ground.

The defeat in Warsaw destroyed the political and military institutions of the Polish underground and left the way open for a Soviet take–over.

With the liberation of Lublin in July 1944 a Russian–sponsored Polish Committee for National Liberation (a Communist Government in all but name) had been set up and the British had put great pressure, mostly unsuccessful, on the Government

–in–exile to accept this status quo. At Yalta, in February 1945, the Allies put Poland within the Russian zone of influence in a post –war Europe. To most Poles the meaning of these two events was perfectly clear; Poland had been betrayed. At one stage the Polish Army, still fighting in Italy and Germany, was prepared to with-draw from the front lines in protest; after all, they were supposed to be fighting for Polish liberation. It is a reflection on Polish honour that no such withdrawal took place since it could leave large gaps in the front lines and so was considered too dangerous for their Allied comrades–in–arms.

The war ended on May 8th, 1945.

Cost of the war for the Poles:

The Poles are the people who really lost the war.

Over half a million fighting men and women, and 6 million civilians (or 22% of the total population) died. About 50% of these were Polish Christians and 50% were Polish Jews. Approximately 5,384,000, or 89.9% of Polish war losses (Jews and Gentiles) were the victims of prisons, death camps, raids, executions, annihilation of ghettos, epidemics, starvation, excessive work and ill treatment. So many Poles were sent to concentration camps that virtually every family had someone close to them who had been tortured or murdered there.

There were one million war orphans and over half a million invalids.

The country lost 38% of its national assets (Britain 0.8%, France 1.5%). Half the country was swallowed up by the Soviet Union including the two great cultural centres of Lwow and Wilno.

Many Poles could not return to the country for which they has fought because they belonged to the „wrong" political group or came from eastern Poland and had thus become Soviet citizens. Others were arrested, tortured and imprisoned by the Soviet authorities for belonging to the Home Army.

Although „victors" they were not allowed to partake in victory celebrations.

Through fighting „For Our Freedom and Yours" they had exchanged one master for another and were, for many years to come, treated as „the enemy" by the very Allies who had betrayed them at Teheran and Yalta.

This is an extract from *History of Poland* by Mieczyslaw Kasprzyk.

2. THE KHAZAKS AND KAZAKHSTAN

Khazakhs (free man in Turkish) originated from nomadic Turkish tribes which settled down in the 15th century round Lake Baikal. During the 17th century they organised themselves in the three HORDES.

The Grand Horde in south of Lake Baikal.

The Middle Horde between the Lake and the Aral Sea.

The Little Horde between the Aral Sea and the river Oura.

At the beginning of the 17th century during the invasion of Dzoungares, certain chiefs called on the Russians for help. As a result The Little Horde passed under Russian protection in 1731 and the other two a few years later. Towards the end of 18th century Russian influence following the infiltration of the hordes sparked many revolts. At the same time, Tartars of Volga spread over the steppes. About this time the Kazakhs converted to Islam. Russian authorities reinforced their positions and deposed the Khan of the Middle Horde in 1822, and then in 1824 the Little Horde and in 1848 the Grande Horde. In 1850 Russians took control of the region in south–east of Lake Baikal. In 1868 there was a great revolt but later relations with the Russians improved as the Kazakh aristocracy showed inclinations towards Russian culture, mainly as a contra balance to Tartar influence. Great colonisation ensued. In 1896 Russian immigration flooded the steppes to the north and east. By 1912 one and a half million of Russian and Ukrainian settlers formed 40% of the population. Kazakhs were confined to the declining areas, especially the arid steppes in the south and the west. The traditional organization started to break up, but 1905 marked the beginning of a nationalistic movement led by Alach Ordais who resisted colonization and the russification. In 1916 the Russian government decided to mobilize 240,000 Muslims of Central Asia to form working battalions.

During the Russian Revolution and the wars between the Red and White Armies the Kazakh resistance collapsed. On 26 August 1920 the Republic of Kirgis (not Kazakhs) was established, forming part of the Soviet Union with Orenburg as the capital. In 1924 it was incorporated in the Republic of Semiretchie with the capital Alma–Ata. In the early twenties the influence of Russian settlers declined, then increased to favour the Kazakh breeders. But the collectivisation introduced in 1928 brought changes forcing people to settle down. There was fierce resistance by the population, leading to executions and massive deportations as well as to a new emigration towards China. At the end of 1930, the Kazakhs population in the republic was only 30%. Soon followed the arrival of deportees.: Koreans in 1931, Poles in 1940 and Volga Germans in 1941. Further difficulties were encountered in 1941 by the Kazakhs when Nikita Khroushchev decided to exploit the good land of Kazakhstan which had not yet been colonised. This provoked a great wave of emigration.

In December 1991 Nursultan Nazarbajev was elected president of the Republic and Kazakhstan has proclaimed its independence, beginning cautiously to develop relationships with the Republics of Central Asia.

Kazakhstan population in 1989 is 16,464,000.
The total area 2,717,000 km^2. Capital is Alma – Ata.

Ethnic breakdown of population :

Kazakhs	–	6, 535.000
Russians	–	6.228.000
Germans	–	958.000
Ukrainians	–	896.000
Uzbeks	–	332.000
Tartars	–	328.000
Uighours	–	185.000
Belorussians	–	183.000
Koreans	–	103.000
Azeris	–	93.000
Poles	–	60.000

Religion: Kazakhs are Sunni Moslems

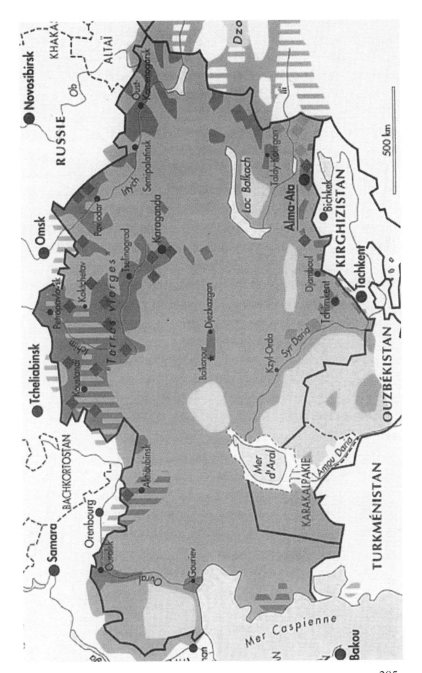

205

3. UGANDA

UGANDA BEFORE 1900

Uganda's strategic position along the central African Rift Valley, its favorable climate at an altitude of 1,200 meters and above, and the reliable rainfall around the Lake Victoria Basin made it attractive to African cultivators and herders as early as the fourth century B. C. Core samples from the bottom of Lake Victoria have revealed that dense rainforest once covered the land around the lake. Centuries of cultivation removed almost all the original tree cover.

The cultivators who gradually cleared the forest were probably Bantu–speaking people, whose slow but inexorable expansion gradually populated most of Africa south of the Sahara Desert. Their knowledge of agriculture and use of iron technology permitted them to clear the land and feed ever larger numbers of settlers. They displaced small bands of indigenous hunter–gatherers, who relocated to the less accessible mountains. Meanwhile, by the fourth century B.C., the Bantu–speaking metallurgists were perfecting iron smelting to produce medium grade carbon steel in preheated forced draft furnaces – a technique not achieved in Europe until the Siemens process of the nineteenth century. Although most of these developments were taking place southwest of modern Ugandan boundaries, iron was mined and smelted in many parts of the country not long afterward.

HISTORICAL LEGACIES AND SOCIAL DIVISIONS

As Uganda's first prime minister, Obote displayed a talent for acting as a broker for groups divided from each other by distance, language, cultural tradition, historical enmities, and rivalries in the form of competing religions–Islam, Roman Catholicism, and Protestantism.

Observers with a powerfully developed sense of hindsight could point to a series of divisions within Ugandan society that contributed to its eventual national disintegration. First, the language gulf between the Nilotic–speaking people of the north and the Bantu–speaking peoples of the south was as wide as that between speakers of Slavic and of Romance languages in Europe. Second, there was an economic divide between the pastoralists, who occupied the drier rangelands of the west and north, and the agriculturists, who cultivated the better–watered highland or lakeside regions. Third, there was a long–standing division between the centralized and sometimes despotic rule of the ancient African kingdoms and the kinship–based politics of recent times, which were characterized by a greater sense of equality and participation. Furthermore, there was a historical political division among the kingdoms themselves. They were often at odds – as in the case of Buganda and Bunyoro and between other pre–colonial polities that disputed control of particular lands. There also were the historical complaints of particular religious groups that had lost ground to rivals in the past: for example, the eclipse of the Muslims at the end of the nineteenth century by Christians allied to British colonialism created an enduring grievance. In addition, Bunyoro's nineteenth–century losses of territory to an expanding Buganda kingdom, allied to British imperialism, gave rise to a problem that would emerge after independence as the „lost counties" issue. Another divisive factor was the uneven development in the colonial period, whereby the south secured railroad transport, cash crops, mission education, and the seat of government, seemingly at the expense of other regions which were still trying to catch up after independence. Another factor was conflicting local nationalism (often misleadingly termed „tribalism"), the most conspicuous example of which was Buganda, whose population of over one million, extensive territory in the favored south of Uganda, and self–proclaimed superiority created a serious backlash among other peoples. Nubians had been brought in from Sudan to serve as a colonial coercive force to suppress local tax revolts. This community shared little sense of identification with

Uganda. The presence of an alien community of professional military people clustered around military encampments added fuel to the fire. And there was another alien community that dominated commercial life in the cities and towns–Asians who had arrived with British colonial rule. Finally, the closely related peoples of nearby Zaire and Sudan soon became embroiled in their own civil wars during the colonial period, drawing in ethnically related Ugandans.

This formidable list of obstacles to national integration, coupled with the absence of nationalist sentiment, left the newly independent Uganda vulnerable to political instability in the 1960's. It was by no means inevitable that the government by consensus and compromise characterizing the early 1960's would devolve into the military near–anarchy of the 1970's. The conditions contributing to such a debacle, however, were already present at independence.

THE ISSUE OF INDEPENDENCE

In 1949 discontented Baganda rioted and burned down the houses of pro–government chiefs. The rioters had three demands: the right to bypass government price controls on the export sales of cotton, the removal of the Asian monopoly over cotton ginning, and the right to have their own representatives in local government replace chiefs appointed by the British. They were critical as well of the young kabaka, Frederick Walugembe Mutesa II (also known as Kabaka Freddie), for his inattention to the needs of his people. The British governor, Sir John Hall, regarded the riots as the work of communist–inspired agitators and rejected the suggested reforms.

Far from leading the people into confrontation, Uganda's would–be agitators were slow to respond to popular discontent. Nevertheless, the Uganda African Farmers Union, founded by I. K. Musazi in 1947, was blamed for the riots and was banned by the British. Musazi's Uganda National Congress replaced the farmers union in 1952, but because the congress remained a casual discussion group more than an organized political party, it stagnated and came to an end just two years after its inception.

Meanwhile, the British began to move ahead of the Ugandans in preparing for independence. The effects of Britain's postwar withdrawal from India, the march of nationalism in West Africa, and a more liberal philosophy in the Colonial Office geared toward future self–rule all began to be felt in Uganda. The embodiment of these issues arrived in 1952 in the person of a new and energetic reformist governor, Sir Andrew Cohen (formerly under-secretary for African affairs in the Colonial Office). Cohen set about preparing Uganda for independence. On the economic side, he removed obstacles to African cotton ginning, rescinded price discrimination against African–grown coffee, encouraged cooperatives, and established the Uganda Development Corporation to promote and finance new projects. On the political side, he reorganized the Legislative Council, which had consisted of an unrepresentative selection of interest groups heavily favoring the European community, to include African representatives elected from districts throughout Uganda. This system became a prototype for the future parliament.

THE COLONIAL ERA

Although momentous change occurred during the colonial era in Uganda, some characteristics of late–nineteenth century African society survived to reemerge at the time of independence. Colonial rule affected local economic systems dramatically, in part because the first concern of the British was financial. Quelling the 1897 mutiny had been costly–units of the Indian army had been transported to Uganda at considerable expense. The new commissioner of Uganda in 1900, Sir Harry H. Johnston, had orders to establish an efficient administration and to levy taxes as quickly as possible. Johnston approached the chiefs in Buganda with offers of jobs in the colonial administration in return for their collaboration. The chiefs, whom Johnston characterized in demeaning terms, were more interested in preserving Buganda as a self–governing entity, continuing the royal line of kabakas, and securing private land tenure for themselves and their supporters. Hard bargaining ensued, but the chiefs ended up with everything they wanted, including one–half of all the land in Buganda. The half left to the British as „Crown Land" was later found to be largely swamp and scrub.

Johnston's Buganda Agreement of 1900 imposed a tax on huts and guns, designated the chiefs as tax collectors, and testified to the continued alliance of British and Baganda interests. The British signed much less generous treaties with the other kingdoms (Toro in 1900, Ankole in 1901, and Bunyoro in 1933) without the provision of large–scale private land tenure. The smaller chiefdoms of Busoga were ignored.

The Baganda immediately offered their services to the British as administrators over their recently conquered neighbors, an offer which was attractive to the economy–minded colonial administration. Baganda agents fanned out as local tax collectors and labor organizers in areas such as Kigezi, Mbale, and, significantly, Bunyoro. This sub–imperialism and Ganda cultural chauvinism were resented by the people being administered. Wherever they went, Baganda insisted on the exclusive use of their language, Luganda, and they planted bananas as the only proper food worth eating. They regarded their traditional dress –long cotton gowns called kanzus–as civilized; all else was barbarian. They also encouraged and engaged in mission work, attempting to convert locals to their form of Christianity or Islam. In some areas, the resulting backlash aided the efforts of religious rivals–for example, Catholics won converts in areas where oppressive rule was identified with a Protestant Muganda chief.

The people of Bunyoro were particularly aggrieved, having fought the Baganda and the British; having a substantial section of their heartland annexed to Buganda as the „lost counties;" and finally having „arrogant" Baganda administrators issuing orders, collecting taxes, and forcing unpaid labor. In 1907 the Banyoro rose in a rebellion called nyangire, or „refusing", and succeeded in having the Baganda sub–imperial agents withdrawn.

Meanwhile, in 1901 the completion of the Uganda railroad from the coast at Mombasa to the Lake Victoria port of Kisumu moved colonial authorities to encourage the growth of cash crops to help pay the railroad's operating costs. Another result of the railroad construction was the 1902 decision to transfer the eastern section of the Uganda Protectorate to the Kenya Colony, then called the East African Protectorate, to keep the entire railroad line under one local colonial administration. Because the railroad experienced cost overruns in Kenya, the British decided to justify its exceptional expense and pay its operating costs by introducing large–scale European settlement in a vast tract of land that became a center of cash–crop agriculture known as the „white highlands."

In many areas of Uganda, by contrast, agricultural production was placed in the hands of Africans, if they responded to the opportunity. Cotton was the crop of choice, largely because of pressure by the British Cotton Growing Association, textile manufacturers who urged the colonies to provide raw materials for British mills. Even the CMS joined the effort by launching the Uganda Company (managed by a former missionary) to promote cotton planting and to buy and transport the produce.

Buganda, with its strategic location on the lakeside, reaped the benefits of cotton growing. The advantages of this crop were quickly recognized by the Baganda chiefs who had newly acquired freehold estates, which came to be known as mailo land because they were measured in square miles. In 1905 the initial baled cotton export was valued at £200; in 1906, £1,000; in 1907;

£11,000; and in 1908, £52,000. By 1915 the value of cotton exports had climbed to £369,000, and Britain was able to end its subsidy of colonial administration in Uganda, while in Kenya the white settlers required continuing subsidies by the home government.

The income generated by cotton sales made the Buganda kingdom relatively prosperous, compared with the rest of colonial Uganda, although before World War I cotton was also being grown in the eastern regions of Busoga, Lango, and Teso. Many Baganda spent their new earnings on imported clothing, bicycles, metal roofing, and even automobiles. They also invested in their children's educations. The Christian missions emphasized literacy skills, and African converts quickly learned to read and write. By 1911 two popular journals, Ebifa (News) and Munno (Your Friend), were published monthly in Luganda. Heavily supported by African funds, new schools were soon turning out graduating classes at Mengo High School, St. Mary's Kisubi, Namilyango, Gayaza, and King's College Budo–all in Buganda. The chief minister of the Buganda kingdom, Sir Apolo Kagwa, personally awarded a bicycle to the top graduate at King's College Budo, together with the promise of a government job. The schools, in fact, had inherited the educational function formerly performed in the kabaka's palace, where generations of young pages had been trained to become chiefs. Now the qualifications sought were literacy and skills, including typing and English translation.

Two important principles of pre–colonial political life carried over into the colonial era: clientage, whereby ambitious younger office–holders attached themselves to older high–ranking chiefs, and generational conflict, which resulted when the younger generation sought to expel their elders from office in order to replace them. After World War I, the younger aspirants to high office in Buganda became impatient with the seemingly perpetual tenure of Sir Apolo and his contemporaries, who lacked many of the skills that members of the younger generation had acquired through schooling. Calling themselves the Young Baganda Association, members of the new generation attached themselves to the young kabaka, Daudi Chwa, who was the figurehead ruler of Buganda under indirect rule. But Kabaka Daudi never gained real political power, and after a short and frustrating reign, he died at the relatively young age of forty–three.

Far more promising as a source of political support were the British colonial officers, who welcomed the typing and translation skills of school graduates and advanced the careers of their favorites. The contest was decided after World War I, when an influx of British ex–military officers, now serving as district commissioners, began to feel that self–government was an obstacle to good government. Specifically, they accused Sir Apolo and his generation of inefficiency, abuse of power, and failure to keep adequate financial accounts–charges that were not hard to document. Sir Apolo resigned in 1926, at about the same time that a host of elderly Baganda chiefs were replaced by a new genera-tion of officeholders. The Buganda treasury was also audited that year for the first time. Although it was not a nationalist organization, the Young Baganda Association claimed to represent popular African dissatisfaction with the old order. As soon as the younger Baganda had replaced the older generation in office, however, their objections to privilege accompanying power ceased. The pattern persisted in Ugandan politics up to and after independence.

The commoners, who had been laboring on the cotton estates of the chiefs before World War I, did not remain servile. As time passed, they bought small parcels of land from their erstwhile landlords. This land fragmentation was aided by the British, who in 1927 forced the chiefs to limit severely the rents and obligatory labor they could demand from their tenants. Thus the oligarchy of landed chiefs who had emerged with the Buganda Agreement of 1900 declined in importance, and agricultural production shifted to independent smallholders, who grew cotton, and later coffee, for the export market.

Unlike Tanganyika, which was devastated during the pro-longed fighting between Britain and Germany in the East African campaign of World War I, Uganda prospered from wartime agricultural production. After the population losses during the era of conquest and the losses to disease at the turn of the century (particularly the devastating sleeping sickness epidemic of 1900–1906), Uganda's population was growing again. Even the 1930's depression seemed to affect smallholder cash farmers in Uganda less severely than it did the white settler producers in Kenya. Ugandans simply grew their own food until rising prices made export crops attractive again.

Two issues continued to create grievance through the 1930's and 1940's. The colonial government strictly regulated the buying and processing of cash crops, setting prices and reserving the role of intermediary for Asians, who were thought to be more efficient. The British and Asians firmly repelled African attempts to break into cotton ginning. In addition, on the Asian–owned sugar plantations established in the 1920's, labor for sugarcane and other cash crops was increasingly provided by migrants from peripheral areas of Uganda and even from outside Uganda.

INDEPENDENCE: THE EARLY YEARS

Uganda's approach to independence was unlike that of most other colonial territories where political parties had been organized to force self–rule or independence from a reluctant colonial regime. Whereas these conditions would have required local and regional differences to be subordinated to the greater goal of winning independence, in Uganda parties were forced to cooperate with one another, with the prospect of independence already assured. One of the major parties, KY, was even opposed to independence unless its particular separatist desires were met. The UPC–KY partnership represented a fragile alliance of two fragile parties.

In the UPC, leadership was factionalized. Each party functionary represented a local constituency, and most of the constituencies were ethnically distinct. For example, Obote's strength lay among his Langi kin in eastern Uganda; George Magezi represented the local interests of his Banyoro compatriots; Grace S.K. Ibingira's strength was in the Ankole kingdom; and Felix Onama was the northern leader of the largely neglected West Nile District in the northwest corner of Uganda. Each of these regional political bosses and those from the other Uganda regions expected to receive a ministerial post in the new Uganda government, to exercise patronage, and to bring the material fruits of independence to local supporters. Failing these objectives, each was likely either to withdraw from the UPC coalition or realign within it.

Moreover, the UPC had had no effective urban organization before independence, although it was able to mobilize the trade unions, most of which were led by non–Ugandan immigrant workers from Kenya (a situation which contributed to the independent Uganda government's almost immediate hostility toward the trade unions). No common ideology united the UPC, the composition of which ranged from the near reactionary Onama to the radical John Kakonge, leader of the UPC Youth League. As prime minister, Obote was responsible for keeping this loose coalition of divergent interest groups intact. Obote also faced the task of maintaining the UPC's external alliances, primarily the coalition between the UPC and the kabaka, who led Buganda's KY. Obote proved adept at meeting the diverse demands of his many partners in government. He even temporarily acceded to some demands which he found repugnant, such as Buganda's claim for special treatment. This accession led to demands by other kingdoms for similar recognition. The Busoga chiefdoms banded together to claim that they, too, deserved recognition under the rule of their newly defined monarch, the kyabasinga.

Not to be outdone, the Iteso people, who had never recognized a pre–colonial king, claimed the title kingoo for Teso District's political boss, Cuthbert Obwangor. Despite these separatist pressures, Obote's long–term goal was to build a strong central government at the expense of entrenched local interests, especially those of Buganda.

The first major challenge to the Obote government came not from the kingdoms, nor the regional interests, but from the military. In January 1964, units of the Ugandan Army mutinied, demanding higher pay and more rapid promotions (see The First Obote Regime: The Growth of the Military, ch. 5). Minister of Defense Onama, who courageously went to speak to the mutineers, was seized and held hostage. Obote was forced to call in British troops to restore order, a humiliating blow to the new regime. In the aftermath, Obote's government acceded to all the mutineers' demands, unlike the governments of Kenya and Tanganyika, which responded to similar demands with increased discipline and tighter control over their small military forces.

The military then began to assume a more prominent role in Ugandan life. Obote selected a popular junior officer with minimal education, Idi Amin Dada, and promoted him rapidly through the ranks as a personal protégé. As the army expanded, it became a source of political patronage and of potential political power.

Later in 1964, Obote felt strong enough to address the critical issue of the „lost counties", which the British had conveniently postponed until after independence. The combination of patronage offers and the promise of future rewards within the ruling coalition gradually thinned opposition party ranks, as members of parliament „crossed the floor" to join the government benches. After two years of independence, Obote finally acquired enough votes to give the UPC a majority and free himself of the KY coalition. The turning point came when several DP members of parliament (MPs) from Bunyoro agreed to join the government side if Obote would undertake a popular referendum to restore the „lost counties" to Bunyoro. The kabaka, naturally, opposed the plebiscite. Unable to prevent it, he sent 300 armed Baganda veterans to the area to intimidate Banyoro voters. In turn, 2,000 veterans from Bunyoro massed on the frontier. Civil war was averted, and the referendum was held. The vote demonstrated an overwhelming desire by residents in the counties annexed to Buganda in 1900 to be restored to their historic Bunyoro allegiance, which was duly enacted by the new UPC majority despite KY opposition.

This triumph for Obote and the UPC strengthened the central government and threw Buganda into disarray. KY unity was weakened by internal recriminations, after which some KY stalwarts, too, began to „cross the floor" to join Obote's victorious government. By early 1966, the result was a parliament composed of seventy–four UPC, nine DP, eight KY, and one independent MP. Obote's efforts to produce a one–party state with a powerful executive prime minister appeared to be on the verge of success.

Paradoxically, however, as the perceived threat from Buganda diminished, many non–Baganda alliances weakened. And as the possibility of an opposition DP victory faded, the UPC coalition itself began to come apart. The one–party state did not signal the end of political conflict, however; it merely relocated and intensified that conflict within the party. The issue that brought the UPC disharmony to a crisis involved Obote's military protégé, Idi Amin.

In 1966 Amin caused a commotion when he walked into a Kampala bank with a gold bar (bearing the stamp of the government of the Belgian Congo) and asked the bank manager to exchange it for cash. Amin's account was ultimately credited with a deposit of £17,000. Obote rivals questioned the incident, and it emerged that the prime minister and a handful of close associates had used Colonel Amin and units of the Uganda Army to intervene in the neighboring Congo crisis. Former supporters of

Congolese leader Patrice Lumumba, led by a „General Olenga", opposed the American–backed government and were attempting to lead the Eastern Province into secession. These troops were reported to be trading looted ivory and gold for arms supplies secretly smuggled to them by Amin. The arrangement became public when Olenga later claimed that he failed to receive the promised munitions. This claim appeared to be supported by the fact that in mid–1965, a seventy–five–ton shipment of Chinese weapons was intercepted by the Kenyan government as it was being moved from Tanzania to Uganda.

Obote's rivals for leadership within the UPC, supported by some Baganda politicians and others who were hostile to Obote, used the evidence revealed by Amin's casual bank deposit to claim that the prime minister and his closest associates were corrupt and had conducted secret foreign policy for personal gain, in the amount of £25,000 each. Obote denied the charge and said the money had been spent to buy the munitions for Olenga's Congolese troops. On February 4, 1966, while Obote was away on a trip to the north of the country, an effective „no confidence" vote against Obote was passed by the UPC Mps. This attempt to remove Obote appeared to be organized by UPC Secretary General Grace S. K. Ibingira, closely supported by the UPC leader from Bunyoro, George Magezi, and a number of other southern UPC notables. Only the radical UPC member, John Kakonge, voted against the motion.

Because he was faced with a nearly unanimous disavowal by his governing party and national parliament, many people expected Obote to resign. Instead, Obote turned to Idi Amin and the army, and, in effect, carried out a coup d'état against his own government in order to stay in power. Obote suspended the constitution, arrested the offending UPC ministers, and assumed control of the state. He forced a new constitution through parliament without a reading and without the necessary quorum.

That constitution abolished the federal powers of the kingdoms, most notably the internal autonomy enjoyed by Buganda, and concentrated presidential powers in the prime minister's office. The kabaka objected, and Buganda prepared to wage a legal battle. Baganda leaders rhetorically demanded that Obote's „illegal" government remove itself from Buganda soil.

Buganda, however, once again miscalculated, for Obote was not interested in negotiating. Instead, he sent Idi Amin and loyal troops to attack the kabaka's palace on nearby Mengo Hill. The palace was defended by a small group of bodyguards armed with rifles and shotguns. Amin's troops had heavy weapons but were reluctant to press the attack until Obote became impatient and demanded results. By the time the palace was overrun, the kabaka had taken advantage of a cloudburst to exit over the rear wall. He hailed a passing taxi and was driven off to exile. After the assault, Obote was reasonably secure from open opposition. The new republican 1967 constitution abolished the kingdoms altogether. Buganda was divided into four districts and ruled through martial law, a forerunner of the military domination over the civilian population that all of Uganda would experience after 1971.

Obote's success in the face of adversity reclaimed for him the support of most members of the UPC, which then became the only legal political party. The original independence election of 1962, therefore, was the last one held in Uganda until December 1980. On the home front, Obote issued the „Common Man's Charter", echoed the call for African Socialism by Tanzanian President Julius Nyerere, and proclaimed a „move to the left" to signal new efforts to consolidate power. His critics noted, however, that he placed most control over economic nationalization in the hands of an Asian millionaire who was also a financial backer of the UPC. Obote created a system of secret police, the General Service Unit (GSU). Headed by a relative, Akena Adoko, the GSU reported on suspected subversives (see Internal Security Services, ch. 5). The Special Force Units of paramilitary police, heavily recruited from Obote's own region and ethnic group, supplemented the security forces within the army and police.

Although Buganda had been defeated and occupied by the military, Obote was still concerned about security there. His concerns were well founded; in December 1969 he was wounded in an assassination attempt and narrowly escaped more serious injury when a grenade thrown near him failed to explode. He had retained power by relying on Idi Amin and the army, but it was not clear that he could continue to count on their loyalty.

Obote appeared particularly uncertain of the army after Amin's sole rival among senior army officers, Brigadier Acap Okoya, was murdered early in 1970. (Amin later promoted the man rumored to have recruited Okoya's killers.) A second attempt was made on Obote's life when his motorcade was ambushed later that year, but the vice–president's car was mistakenly riddled with bullets. Obote began to recruit more Acholi and Langi troops, and he accelerated their promotions to counter the large numbers of soldiers from Amin's home, which was then known as West Nile District. Obote also enlarged the paramilitary Special Force as a counterweight to the army.

Amin, who at times inspected his troops wearing an outsized sport shirt with Obote's face across the front and back, protested his loyalty. But in October 1970, Amin was placed under temporary house arrest while investigators looked into his army expenditures, reportedly several million dollars over budget. Another charge against Amin was that he had continued to aid southern Sudan's Anya Nya rebels in opposing the regime of Jafaar Numayri even after Obote had shifted his support away from the Anyanya to Numayri. This foreign policy shift provoked an outcry from Israel, which had been supplying the Anyanya rebels. Amin was close friends with several Israeli military advisers who were in Uganda to help train the Ugandan Army, and their eventual role in Amin's efforts to oust Obote remained the subject of continuing controversy.

4. UNRRA – UNHCR

UNRA – UNHCR

The United Nations High Commissioner for Refuges was established by the U.N. General Assembly in 1950, one of the several attempts by the international community during the 20th century to provide protection and assistance to refugees. The League of Nations, the forerunner of the U.N., had named Norwegian scientist and explorer Fridtjof Nansen to the post of High Commissioner as early as 1921. World War II provided the impetus for several organisations, the United Nations Relief and Rehabilitation Agency (UNRRA), the International Refugee Organisation and subsequently UNHCR.

The new agency was given a limited three–year mandate to help resettle 1.2 million European refugees left homeless by the global conflict. But as refugee crises mushroomed around the globe, its mandate was extended every five years. Today, UNHCR is one of the world's principal humanitarian agencies, its staff of more then 5,000 personnel helping 19.8 million people in more then 120 countries. During its half century of work, the agency provided assistance to at least 50 million people, earning two Nobel Peace Prizes in 1954 and 1981.

UNHCR's programme, its protection and other policy guidelines, are approved by an Executive Committee of 61 member states which meets annually in Geneva. A second "working group" or Standing Committee meets several times a year. The High Commissioner reports on the results of the agency's work annually to the U.N. Genèral Assembly through the Economic and Social Council.